Name: Naila Parisa
Class: Mr. White
5th Grade

READING/WRITING COMPANION

Naila

COVER: Nathan Love, Erwin Madrid

mheducation.com/prek-12

Send all inquiries to:
McGraw-Hill Education
Two Penn Plaza
New York, NY 10121

ISBN: 978-0-07-901841-0
MHID: 0-07-901841-6

Printed in the United States of America.

9 10 11 12 13 14 15 SWI 26 25 24 23 22 B

Welcome to Wonders!

Read exciting Literature, Science, and Social Studies texts!

- ★ LEARN about the world around you!
- ★ THINK, SPEAK, and WRITE about genres!
- ★ COLLABORATE in discussion and inquiry!
- ★ EXPRESS yourself!

MR. PRESIDENT HOW LONG MUST WOMEN WAIT FOR LIBERTY

my.mheducation.com

Use your student login to read core texts, practice grammar and spelling, explore research projects and more!

(t) Buena Vista Images/Stone/Getty Images; (c) Everett Collection/SuperStock; (bl) Rubberball/Nicole Hill/Getty Images; (bc) wong sze yuen/Shutterstock.com; (br) vipman/Shutterstock.com

UNIT 5

GENRE STUDY 1 EXPOSITORY TEXT

SCIENCE

GENRE STUDY 2 HISTORICAL FICTION

GENRE STUDY 3 ARGUMENTATIVE TEXT

SCIENCE

WRAP UP THE UNIT

SOCIAL STUDIES SCIENCE

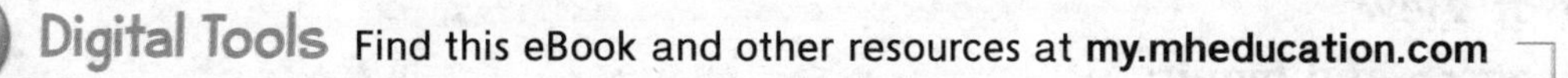

Digital Tools Find this eBook and other resources at **my.mheducation.com**

UNIT 6

GENRE STUDY 1 **HISTORICAL FICTION**

SOCIAL STUDIES

GENRE STUDY 2 **EXPOSITORY TEXT**

SCIENCE

Lophelia II 2009 Expedition, NOAA-OER

GENRE STUDY 3 **POETRY**

WRAP UP THE UNIT

Digital Tools Find this eBook and other resources at **my.mheducation.com**

Talk About It

Essential Question

How can scientific knowledge change over time?

Learning about the ocean is one of our greatest challenges. As researchers design new technologies and evaluate new ideas, our criteria for knowledge may change.

Look at the photo. It shows a submersible that can take people deep under the ocean. Talk with a partner about how new scientific discoveries and inventions help to change the scientific knowledge we have. Think about how they have affected your own life. Write your ideas in the web.

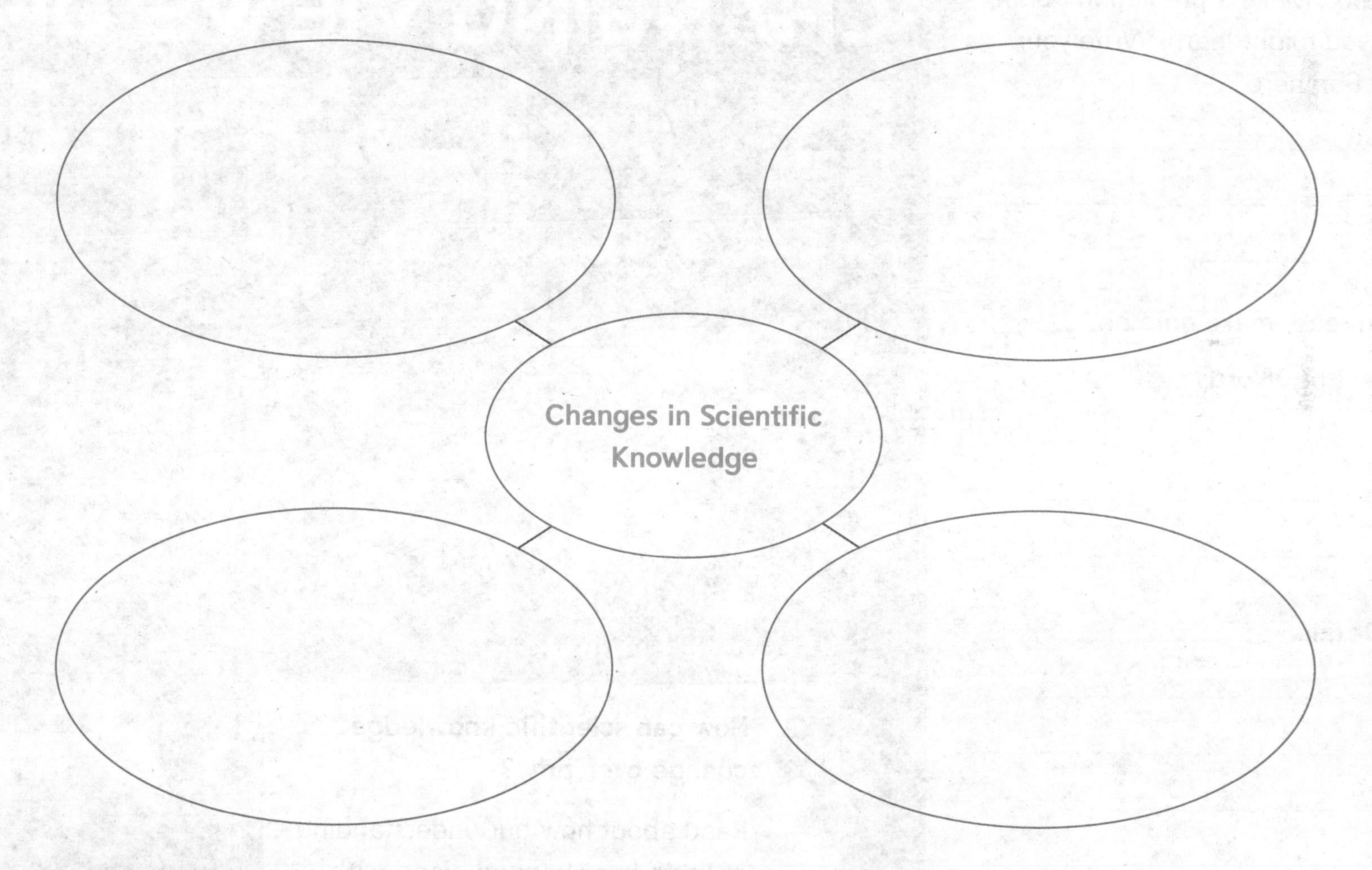

Go online to **my.mheducation.com** and read the "A Better World with Satellites" Blast. Think about how scientific knowledge has changed over time. How has new technology affected our world? Then blast back your response.

SHARED READ

TAKE NOTES

Previewing text helps you get an idea of what it will be about. Before you read, look at the headings and diagrams. Make a prediction about what you might learn. Write your prediction here.

____

____

____

As you read, make note of:

Interesting Words ______________________

____

____

____

Key Details ______________________

____

____

____

____

____

____

CHANGING VIEWS OF EARTH

Essential Question

How can scientific knowledge change over time?

Read about how our understanding of Earth has changed along with scientific developments over time.

On the Ground, Looking Around

No matter where on Earth you go, people like to talk about the weather. This weekend's forecast may provide the main **criteria** for planning outdoor activities. Where does all that information about the weather come from? The ability to predict storms and droughts required centuries of scientific innovation. We had to look up at the skies to learn more about life here on Earth.

Long ago, humans based their knowledge on what they experienced with their eyes and ears. If people could heighten their senses, they might not feel so mystified by the events confronting them daily. For example, something as simple as the rising sun perplexed people for centuries. They believed that the Earth stayed in place while the Sun moved around it. This was called the geocentric model.

In the early 1600s, an Italian named Galileo pointed a new tool called the telescope toward the night sky. As a result of his heightened vision, he could see stars, planets, and other celestial **spheres** with new clarity. Each observation and **calculation** led him to support a radical new model of the solar system. In the heliocentric version proposed by the scientist Copernicus, the Sun did not **orbit** the Earth. The Earth orbited the Sun.

Galileo's telescope helped prove that Copernicus's heliocentric view was correct. ▶

These diagrams show the geocentric (Earth in the center), and the heliocentric (Sun in the center) views of the solar system.

Hulton Archive/Getty Images

EXPOSITORY TEXT

FIND TEXT EVIDENCE

Read

Paragraphs 1-2

Ask and Answer Questions

Why did people long ago think the Sun moved around the Earth? **Underline** the text evidence and write the answer here.

____

____

____

____

Paragraph 3

Cause and Effect

Circle the text evidence that explains how the telescope helped Galileo. **Draw a box** around the clue words that tell you the telescope had an effect in helping Galileo.

Reread

Author's Craft

How does the author help you understand the difference between the geocentric and heliocentric model of the solar system?

SHARED READ

FIND TEXT EVIDENCE

Read

Paragraphs 1-2

Ask and Answer Questions

What is a question you can ask and answer about measurement devices? Write the question and **underline** the answer.

____

____

Paragraphs 3-4

Cause and Effect

Circle the effects aircraft had on advancing the study of weather patterns.

Diagram

At what altitude do the Troposphere and Tropopause meet?

____

Author's Craft

Why is "In the Sky, Looking Down" a good heading for this section?

In the Sky, Looking Down

New technology allowed scientists to **evaluate** theories better than ever. Measuring devices such as the thermometer and barometer offered new insights into weather patterns. However, people were still limited to ground-based learning. What if they could travel into the sky, where the weather actually happened?

In the mid-1700s, some scientists sent measurement devices higher and higher. At first they used kites. Before long, hot-air balloons offered new ways to **transport** the tools–and sometimes scientists themselves–into the sky.

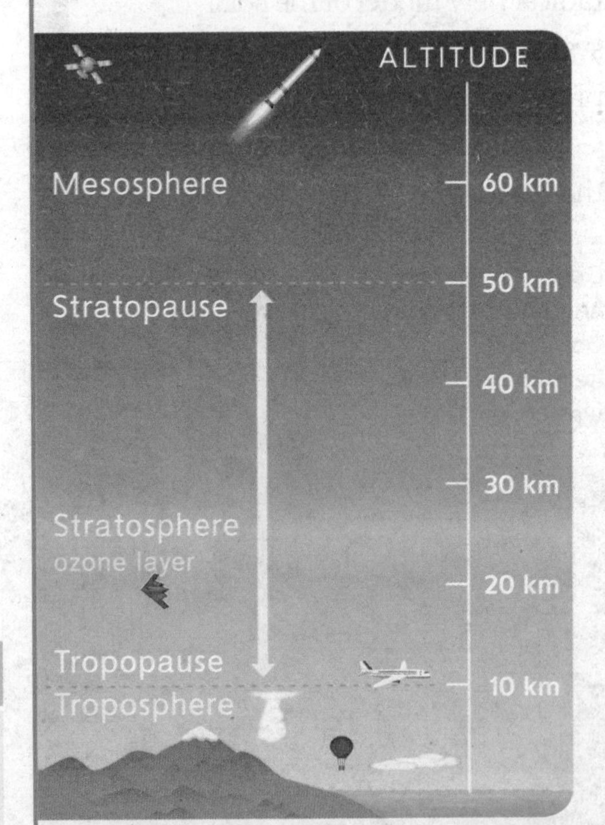

As humans reached higher, we learned more and more about Earth's atmosphere.

However, scientists were not satisfied studying the lower layers of Earth's atmosphere. The more they learned, the higher they wanted to go. They also wanted to obtain information more quickly and accurately. Kites and balloons were hard to control. As a result, they occasionally veered off course or got lost, taking their data with them.

The development of aircraft in the early 1900s promised safer ways to observe Earth's surface and the atmosphere above it. Kites and balloons could reach altitudes of **approximately** three kilometers. By comparison, airplanes lifted scientists to a height of five kilometers and more. Radio technology allowed scientists to transmit data from the air to the ground, where other scientists analyzed and compared information. Breakthroughs came fast and furiously. Still, scientists dreamed of reaching ever higher.

Out in Space, Looking Back Home

In the late twentieth century, advances in aeronautics led to more powerful rockets that lifted satellites into orbit around Earth. From these heights, scientists could study the composition and relative thinness of our layered atmosphere. Since meteorologists could analyze multiple factors at once, the accuracy of their weather predictions improved dramatically.

NASA launched dozens of satellites into orbit in the following years. Some stared back at Earth, while others peered deep into endless space. They gathered **astronomical** data about the ages of planets and galaxies. Sensors and supercomputers measured things such as Earth's **diameter** with incredible accuracy. Because of this technology, scientists could develop more reliable models about Earth's systems. For example, they could form theories to show how climate might change over time.

Space missions continue to venture farther from home. Even so, nothing compares to seeing Earth the old way, with our own eyes. Views of our planet from space inspire awe in nearly all people who have seen them, even in photographs. "With all the arguments . . . for going to the Moon," said astronaut Joseph Allen, "no one suggested that we should do it to look at the Earth. But that may in fact be the most important reason."

Satellites launched into orbit only last for a limited number of years and then must be replaced.

Summarize

Use your notes to write a short summary of the important information in "Changing Views of Earth." Talk about whether the prediction you made before reading was confirmed.

EXPOSITORY TEXT

FIND TEXT EVIDENCE

Read

Paragraphs 1-3

Greek Roots

How does the Greek root *photo*, meaning "light," help you understand more about how *photographs* are created?

___

___

___

Evaluate Information

Underline Joseph Allen's quote. Do you think Allen is qualified to say this? Why or why not?

___

___

___

Reread

Author's Craft

How does the author use text structure to help you understand how the ability to predict weather improved in the late 20th century?

Vocabulary

Use the example sentences to talk with a partner about each word. Then answer the questions.

approximately

The recipe called for **approximately** two cups of oil, so I did not measure exactly.

What is an antonym, or the opposite, of approximately?

astronomical

At the space exhibit, we used **astronomical** instruments to look at the Moon.

What else can you study with astronomical instruments?

calculation

Mina did a **calculation** to see if she had enough money to buy six tickets.

What is one skill that would help with a calculation?

criteria

Blood pressure is one of the **criteria** doctors use to check your health.

What other criteria can doctors use to check your health?

diameter

A large pizza pan has a **diameter** of fourteen inches.

What could you use to measure the diameter of a pan?

Build Your Word List Pick a word you found interesting in the selection you read. Look up synonyms and antonyms of the word in a thesaurus and write them in your writer's notebook.

evaluate

Reading a food label can help you **evaluate** whether the food has good nutrition.

How can you evaluate a book you have read?

___

___

orbit

It takes one year for the Earth to **orbit** the Sun.

What other objects in space orbit the Sun?

___

___

___

spheres

Basketballs and baseballs are **spheres,** but footballs are not.

What other objects are spheres?

___

___

___

Greek Roots

Many English words have Greek roots. The Greek root *geo* means "earth," so any English word that has the word part *geo,* like *geocentric,* usually has to do with the planet Earth.

FIND TEXT EVIDENCE

On page 3 of "Changing Views of Earth," I come across the word geocentric. *The Greek root* centr *means* "center." *Since I know that* geo *means "earth," I can figure out that something that is geocentric means "Earth centered." The diagram that shows the Earth in the center with the Sun and planets traveling around it must be the* geocentric *model.*

They believed that the Earth stayed in place while the Sun moved around it. This was called the geocentric model.

Your Turn Use the Greek roots below to figure out the meanings of two words from "Changing Views of Earth."

Greek Roots: helio = sun therm = heat
meter = measure

heliocentric, *page 3* ___

thermometer, *page 4* ___

Ask and Answer Questions

Asking and answering questions as you read helps you to deepen your understanding of the text. Try it with "Changing Views of Earth." Think about each question the author asks, and generate your own questions, too. Then read on for the answers. After you have finished reading, think about more questions related to the topic that you might have.

Quick Tip

You can write a comment about information in the margin of your own book, or you can use a sticky note in other books. This will help you remember the important information. Writing a comment is called *annotating.* Annotating can help you better understand what you are reading.

FIND TEXT EVIDENCE

In the first paragraph on page 3, the author asks a question:

Where does all that information about the weather come from? This may lead you to another question.

Page 3

> No matter where on Earth you go, people like to talk about the weather. This weekend's forecast may provide the main **criteria** for planning outdoor activities. Where does all that information about the weather come from?

I think about what I already know—that weather forecasters use scientific instruments. So I ask myself, "What kinds of instruments do scientists use to make forecasts?" I will read on to find the answer.

Your Turn Reread "Out in Space, Looking Back Home" on page 5. Ask a question and then read to find the answer. Use the strategy Ask and Answer Questions as you read. Write your question and answer below.

____

____

Diagrams

The selection "Changing Views of Earth" is an expository text. Expository text presents information and facts about a topic in a logical order. It often includes a variety of text structures to support points with reasons and evidence. It may also include text features, such as subheadings, photos, and diagrams.

Readers to Writers

Writers use diagrams to illustrate important information in the text. When might you use a diagram in your own writing?

FIND TEXT EVIDENCE

"Changing Views of Earth" is an expository text. The facts about inventions are given in a logical order. The author backs up her points with evidence, including diagrams.

Page 4

In the Sky, Looking Down

New technology allowed scientists to **evaluate** theories better than ever. Measuring devices such as the thermometer and barometer offered new insights into weather patterns. However, people were still limited to ground-based learning. What if they could travel into the sky, where the weather actually happened?

In the mid-1700s, some scientists sent measurement devices higher and higher. At first they used kites. Before long, hot-air balloons offered new ways to **transport** the tools—and sometimes scientists themselves—into the sky.

However, scientists were not satisfied studying the lower layers of Earth's atmosphere. The more they learned, the higher they wanted to go. They also wanted to obtain information more quickly and accurately. Kites and balloons were hard to control. As a result, they occasionally veered off course or got lost, taking their data with them.

The development of aircraft in the early 1900s promised safer ways to observe Earth's surface and the atmosphere above it. Kites and balloons could reach altitudes of **approximately** three kilometers. By comparison, airplanes lifted scientists to a height of five kilometers and more. Radio technology allowed scientists to transmit data from the air to the ground, where other scientists analyzed and compared information. Breakthroughs came fast and furiously. Still, scientists dreamed of reaching ever higher.

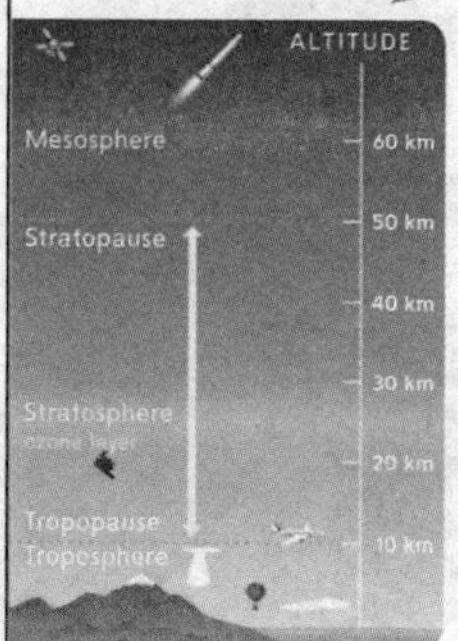

As humans reached higher, we learned more and more about Earth's atmosphere.

Diagrams

A diagram is a drawing that shows the different parts of something and how the parts relate to one another. Labels identify different parts of the diagram.

Your Turn Review and discuss why "Changing Views of Earth" is an expository text. How is the information in the two diagrams helpful?

____

____

____

____

Cause and Effect

Science and history authors want you to know not just *what* happens but why it happens. They show that one event is the **cause** of another event, called the **effect.** Sometimes, the effect of one event becomes the cause of another event.

FIND TEXT EVIDENCE

In the section "On the Ground, Looking Around" on page 3, I read that people once believed the Sun orbits Earth. I learned the cause of this mistake: people had only their eyes for viewing the skies. The invention of the telescope had an important effect—the discovery that Earth actually orbits the Sun.

Cause	→	Effect
Long ago, people had only their eyes to see the skies.	→	They thought the Sun orbited Earth.
The telescope was invented.	→	People could see the stars and planets more clearly.
People could see the stars and planets more clearly.	→	They found out that Earth orbits the Sun.

Quick Tip

These words signal cause-and-effect relationships.

Cause: *because, if, since, led to*

Effect: *as a result, then, finally, so, therefore, for this reason*

Hulton Archive/Getty Images

Your Turn Show important connections between certain events in "Changing Views of Earth" by recording causes and effects in your graphic organizer.

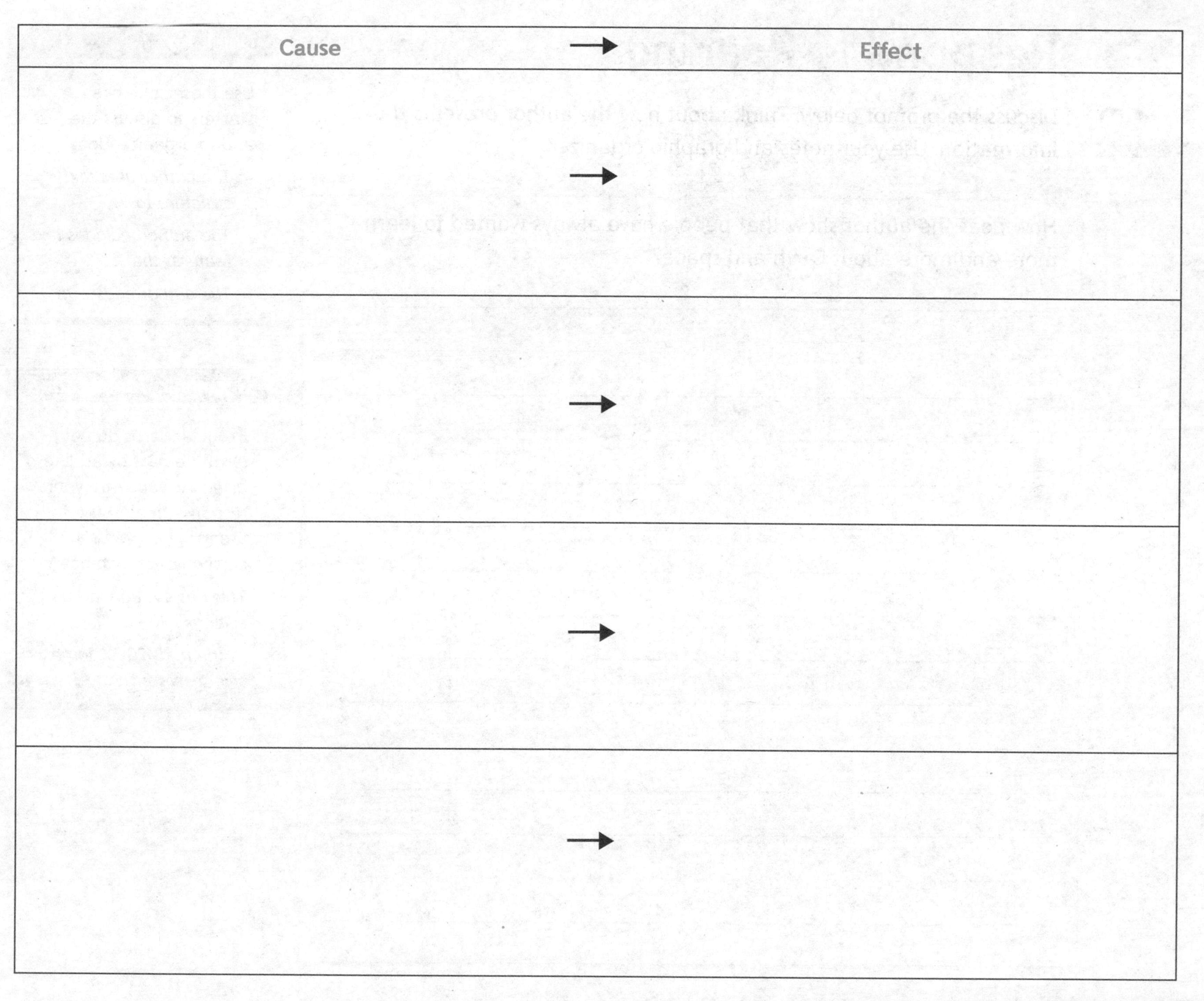

Cause	→	Effect
	→	
	→	
	→	
	→	

Respond to Reading

Discuss the prompt below. Think about how the author presents the information. Use your notes and graphic organizer.

How does the author show that people have always wanted to learn more and more about Earth and space?

Quick Tip

Use these sentence starters to discuss the text and to organize ideas.

- *The author uses text structure to. . .*
- *The author includes text features that. . .*
- *The author ends with. . .*

Grammar Connections

Irregular verbs do not form the past by adding *d* or *ed*. As you write your response, make sure to use irregular verbs correctly. For instance:

*This observation **led** scientists to. . .*

*In the mid-1700s, some scientists **sent**. . .*

SCIENCE

Paraphrasing Sources

Paraphrasing means restating, or giving, the source's information in your own words. The meaning of the information stays the same.

Plagiarism is copying an author's exact words and using them as your own. You should never plagiarize. You can avoid plagiarism by paraphrasing a source. If you quote an author's exact words, be sure to give the source. Here is an example: On page 4 of "Changing Views of Earth" the text states, "Kites and balloons were hard to control." Paraphrase the quote from the text.

____

____

____

original text

The ability to predict storms and droughts required centuries of scientific innovation.

paraphrased text

It took centuries of scientific innovations to be able to predict storms and droughts.

How is the second text a paraphrase of the original?

____

____

____

____

____

____

Create a Podcast With a group, create a podcast that explains the relationship of the Earth, Sun, and Moon. You can add music and sound effects. Consider these questions when looking for information:

- How are the physical characteristics different?
- What does the Sun provide the Earth?
- How does the Moon affect the Earth?

Discuss what reliable sources you might use in your research. After you finish, you will share your podcast with classmates. Be careful not to plagiarize any information presented. Tell what your sources are at the end of the podcast.

Reread | ANCHOR TEXT

When Is a Planet Not a Planet?

Literature Anthology: pages 346–361

How does the author use the first part of "Pluto's Problems" to support her ideas about different groups of planets?

Talk About It Reread **Literature Anthology** page 349. Turn to a partner and discuss how the information in the section is organized.

Cite Text Evidence What information does the author want you to know about planets? Write text evidence in the chart.

Inner Planets	Outer Planets

Write The author supports her ideas about different groups of plants in "Pluto's Problems" by ______________________________

____

____

____

____

Synthesize Information

Combine what you already know about planets with the information in the text in order to better understand how the author supports her ideas. Remember to also look at the information in the illustrations and caption.

How does the author use diagrams to help you understand more about the solar system?

Talk About It Reread the diagram and caption on page 352 in the **Literature Anthology**. Turn to your partner and discuss how the diagram connects to the main text.

Cite Text Evidence How does including the diagram support the ideas the author is developing? Cite text evidence from the diagram.

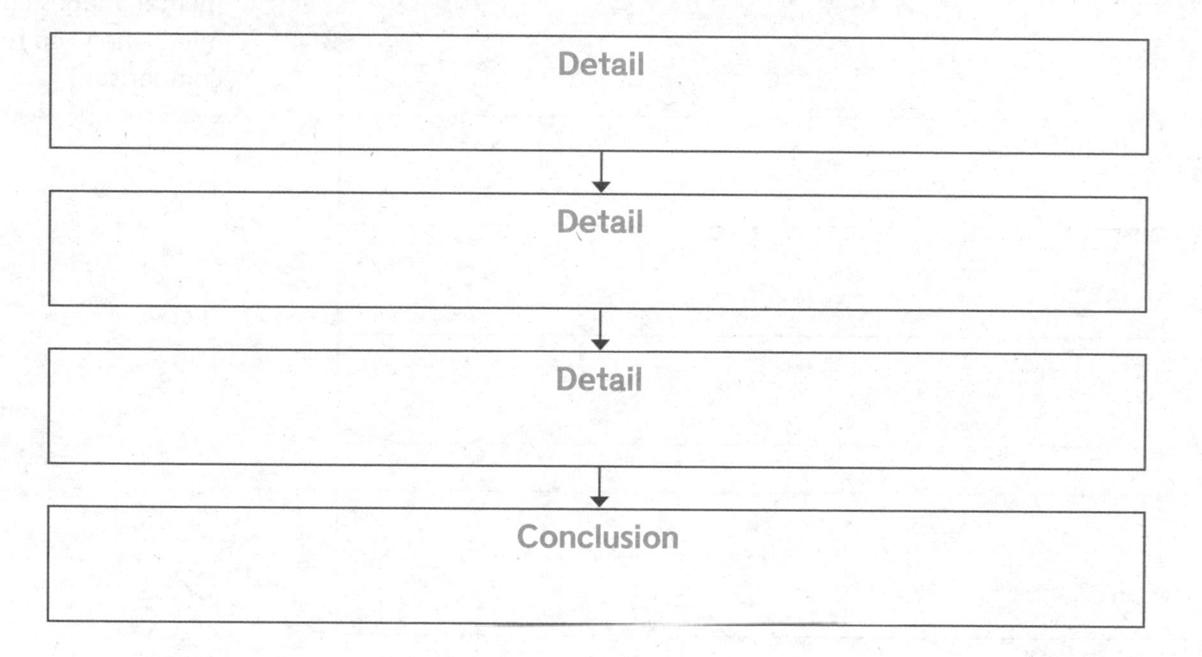

Write The author uses the solar system diagram to help me understand

____

____

____

____

Quick Tip

Use these sentence starters to talk about the diagram.

- *The diagram helps me see. . .*
- *I know that Pluto. . .*

Reread | ANCHOR TEXT

How does the author use the description of a schoolyard bully to help you understand what she means by the phrase "clearing the neighborhood"?

Talk About It Reread **Literature Anthology** page 358. Turn to a partner and talk about what "clearing the neighborhood" means.

Cite Text Evidence What words and phrases tell how some planets are like schoolyard bullies? Write text evidence in the chart.

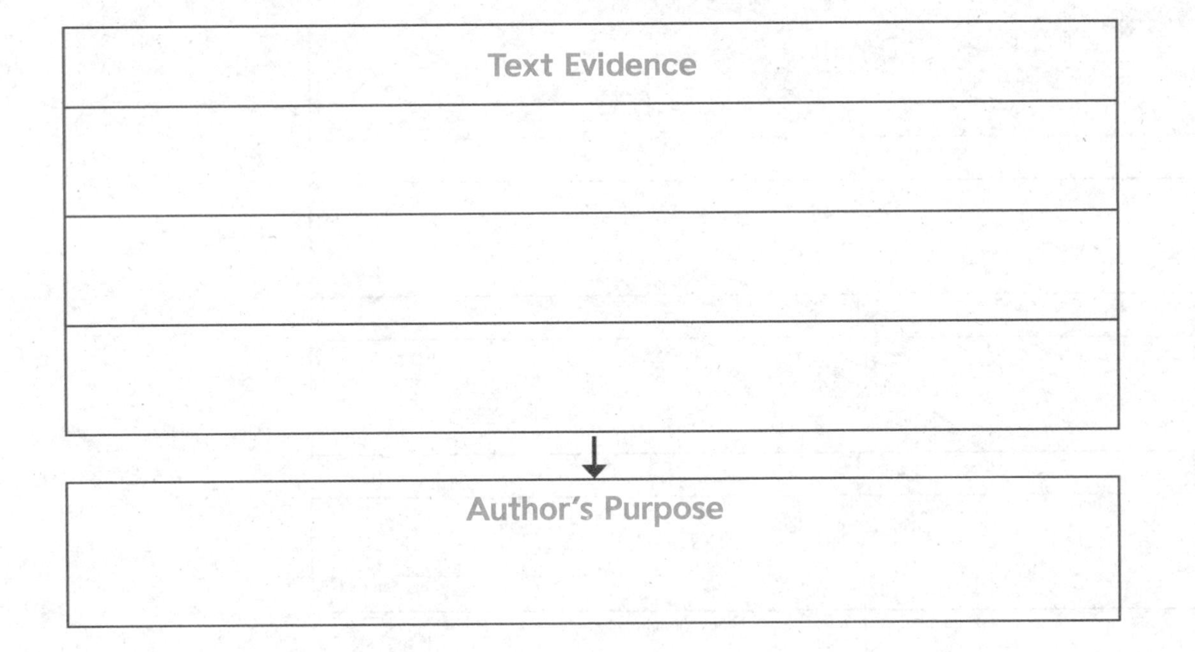

Write The author's description of a schoolyard bully helps me to understand how planets ______________________

____

____

Quick Tip

When you reread, try to picture what the author is saying. This will help to deepen your understanding. For example, the author compares an orbit to a lane on a racetrack. What mental images come to mind when you read this comparison?

Respond to Reading

Discuss the prompt below. Apply your own knowledge about the characteristics of Pluto to inform your answer. Use your notes and graphic organizer.

Think about how the author supports her ideas. How does she use organization and text features to explain Pluto's status as a planet?

Quick Tip

Use these sentence starters to talk about and cite text evidence.

- *The author uses text features to . . .*
- *She organizes information to . . .*
- *The way she supports her ideas helps me to . . .*

Self-Selected Reading

Choose a text and fill in your writer's notebook with the title, author, and genre. Include a personal response to the text in your writer's notebook.

NASA/Johns Hopkins University Applied Physics Laboratory/Southwest Research Institute

Reread | PAIRED SELECTION

The Crow and the Pitcher

Literature Anthology: pages 364–365

1 *A fable is a form of classical literature that usually includes animals as characters and ends with a moral. Aesop was an ancient Greek storyteller who is credited with many fables, now known as Aesop's Fables. His criteria for a good tale seem simple: Tell a meaningful story and end with an unforgettable moral.*

2 A crow, whose throat was parched and dry with thirst, saw a pitcher in the distance. With great joy, he flew to it.

3 The crow found that the pitcher held a little water.

4 He stooped and he strained, but the water was too near the bottom of the pitcher. He could not reach it.

5 Next he tried to overturn the pitcher, thinking that he would be able to catch some of the water as it trickled out.

Reread paragraphs 2, 3, and 4. **Circle** the text evidence that explains the crow's problem. Write your answer here:

Discuss with a partner what the crow did to try to solve his problem. **Underline** the crow's attempts. Talk about what you think the crow might do next.

6 The tired crow was too weak to knock over the pitcher. He took a minute to evaluate the situation and devise a plan.

7 He collected as many stones as he could.

8 He dropped a stone into the pitcher with his beak. Then he peered into the pitcher.

9 He could not tell if his plan was working yet, so he dropped another stone into the pitcher. And then he added another.

10 The crow looked again. "This experiment just might work!" he thought.

11 One by one the crow dropped stones into the pitcher until he brought the water within his reach and thus saved his life.

12 Moral: *Necessity is the mother of invention.*

Reread the text. Make marks next to the additional steps the crow took to save himself.

Reread the moral of the fable. Discuss with your partner what you think it means. Write your ideas below.

Reread | PAIRED SELECTION

How do the crow's actions help convey the author's message?

Reread paragraph 1 on page 18. Think about the characteristics of a fable. Discuss with your partner how "The Crow and the Pitcher" fits these characteristics.

Talk About It Reread the excerpts on pages 18 and 19.

Discuss the crow's problem and the moral of the fable.

Cite Text Evidence What do the crow's actions show? Write the text evidence in the chart.

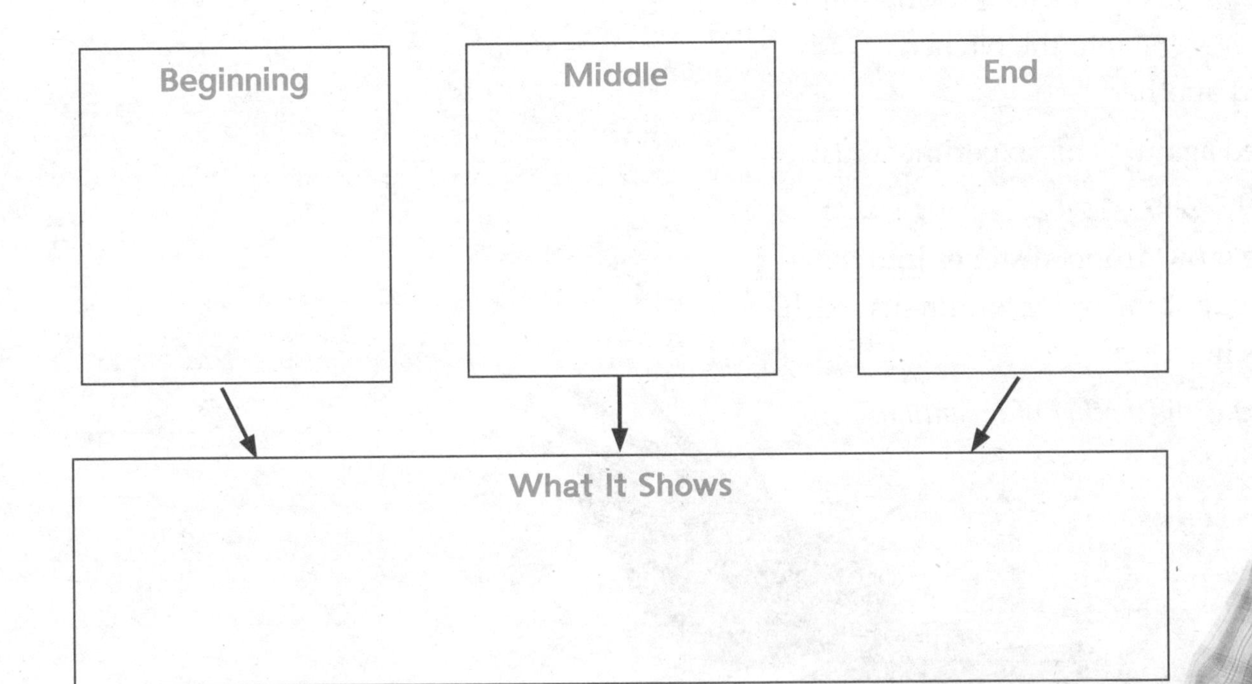

Write The crow's actions convey the author's message by ________

____

____

Imagery

Writers use imagery to help create mental images in a reader's mind. These words and phrases often appeal to the senses to describe what something looks, smells, feels, tastes, and sounds like. Imagery can also affect mood, or the feeling, the writer creates in the reader.

FIND TEXT EVIDENCE

On page 18 of "The Crow and the Pitcher" in paragraph 2, the author says that the crow's throat was "parched and dry with thirst." By using this phrase, the author creates an image that helps readers imagine how their throats would feel if they were suffering from extreme thirst.

> A crow, whose throat was parched and dry with thirst, saw a pitcher in the distance.

Your Turn Reread the rest of page 18 and paragraph 6 on page 19.

- What words does the author use to create imagery? ______________________

____

- How does the author's use of imagery create and maintain the mood of the story? ______________________

____

Readers to Writers

You can use imagery in your writing. Think about what you want your readers to see, hear, touch, smell, or taste. Choose words that create these images. Also think about the mood of your writing. If you want a scary, calm, anxious, or happy mood, choose words and phrases that help to set and maintain this mood.

Text Connections

Quick Tip

Think about what you have read in the selections and in the caption on this page. Talk about how knowledge is gained and what makes people want to gain knowledge.

How do the artist and the authors of *When Is a Planet Not a Planet?* and "The Crow and the Pitcher" help you understand how knowledge can be gained?

Talk About It Look at the painting. Read the caption. Talk with a partner about what you see in the painting.

Cite Text Evidence **Circle** what the artist wants you to focus on. Think about how and why people gain knowledge. Reread the caption and **underline** evidence that helps you understand how a comet inspired scientific knowledge.

Write The artist and authors show how knowledge can be gained by

____

____

____

____

____

____

____

Giovanni Battista Donati discovered this comet over Florence, Italy on June 2, 1858. It was observed and studied by many astronomers. The comet became the subject of newspaper and magazine articles. William Turner's painting captures the comet's curved tail. Donati's comet inspired many scientists and people to learn more about the night sky.

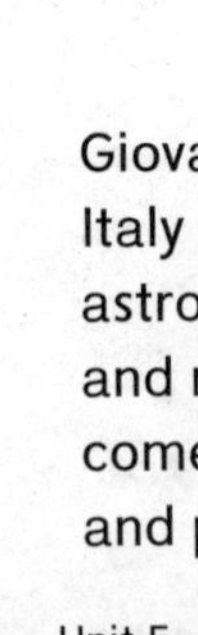

SCIENCE

Present Your Work

COLLABORATE

Discuss how you will present your podcast about the characteristics of the Earth, Sun, and Moon. Use the Presenting Checklist as you practice your presentation. Discuss the sentence starters below and write your answers.

Interesting information that I learned about the characteristics of the Sun, Moon, and Earth includes ______________________________

____

____

____

I would like to know more about ______________________________

____

____

____

Tech Tip

You can present your podcast live to the class. If you are able to record your podcast for your presentation, review the audio to make sure it is clear and easy to understand. You may be able to edit out any interruptions or long pauses.

Presenting Checklist

- ☐ Assign speaking roles within your group. Rehearse your presentation. Provide feedback.
- ☐ Speak slowly, clearly, and with an appropriate volume.
- ☐ Use expression and appropriate tone to show your audience that you have important and interesting ideas to share.
- ☐ Listen actively to comments and questions from the audience.

Literature Anthology: pages 346–361

Expert Model

Features of a Research Report

A research report is an expository text that informs readers about a topic based on relevant information gathered from various sources. A research report

- introduces a topic in an interesting way
- provides an overview of facts, specific details, examples, and explanations gathered from research
- organizes information in a logical order

Word Wise

On page 347, the author begins the introduction to the topic by using language that is entertaining and easy for readers to understand. This helps readers feel that the author is talking to them about a topic she finds interesting.

Analyze an Expert Model Studying expository texts will help you learn how to plan and write a research report. **Reread** the first paragraph of *When Is a Planet Not a Planet?* on page 347 in the **Literature Anthology**. Write your answers to the questions below.

How does the author spark your interest in the topic? Use text evidence.

____

____

____

What specific detail about Mercury and Pluto does the author give?

____

____

Plan: Choose Your Topic

Brainstorm With a partner, brainstorm a list of scientific advancements made in the 21st century. Scientific advancements can include new knowledge and understanding, as well as new inventions. Write your ideas below.

____

____

____

____

____

Quick Tip

If you are unsure which scientific advancements were made in the 21st century, you can ask your teacher for assistance.

To help you choose your topic, think about what you are the most interested in. What do you want to learn about this topic?

Writing Prompt Choose one scientific advancement of the 21st century from your list. Write a research report telling about this advancement. Include why the advancement is important.

I will write about ______________________________.

Purpose and Audience Think about who will read or hear your report. Will your **purpose** be to inform, persuade, or entertain?

My purpose for writing is to ______________________________.

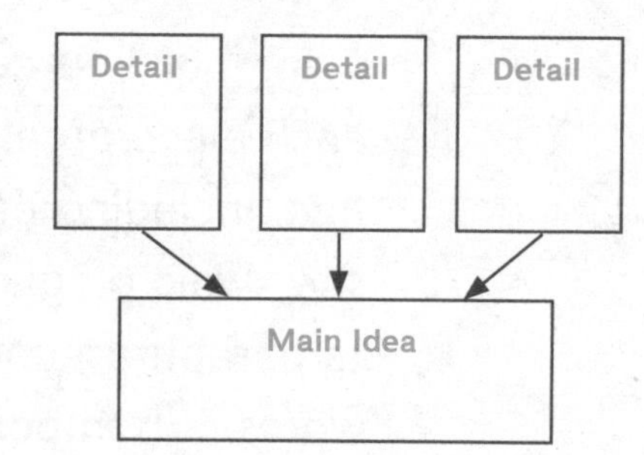

Plan In your writer's notebook, make a Main Idea and Details chart to plan your writing. Fill in the Main Idea with the scientific advancement you have chosen. Fill in the details as you research your topic.

WRITING

Plan: Relevant Information

Choose Relevant Information After you find reliable resources for your report, look for information that is relevant, or relates to your topic. Use the main idea for your topic to help you focus on the information you need. As you read your sources, think about these questions:

- Have I read the source carefully and critically?
- Is this information good evidence for one of my main points?
- Have I used a variety of sources in order to find different kinds of information? Other sources may include additional information.

List two pieces of relevant information for your report.

1. ______________________________

____

2. ______________________________

____

Cite Your Sources Note the source of each piece of relevant information you find, including page number or web site. Avoid plagiarism. Even if you plan to paraphrase information in your own words, it is important to cite the sources you used in your bibliography. Use quotes exactly the way they appear in the source.

Draft

Facts and Specific Details Authors use facts and specific details to support the main ideas in their research reports. In the example below from "Changing Views of Earth," the author gives facts, such as a time period, and specific details, such as "five kilometers," about the height that airplanes could lift scientists.

> The development of aircraft in the early 1900s promised safer ways to observe Earth's surface and the atmosphere above it. Kites and balloons were hard to control. Airplanes lifted scientists to a height of five kilometers and more.

Now use the paragraph as a model to write about the 21st century scientific advancement you chose for your topic. State your main idea.Then provide facts and specific details from your research that are relevant to your main idea.

Write a Draft Use your Main Idea and Details graphic organizer to help you write your draft in your writer's notebook. Don't forget to write an introduction that sparks interest in your topic.

Grammar Connections

Make sure that any pronoun you use relates to the noun, or antecedent, that comes before it. In the excerpt, the pronoun *it* refers to the Earth's surface.

Revise

Logical Order When writers revise their draft, they should make sure that their facts and specific details are presented in a logical order, or sequence, that makes sense. The reader should be able to follow the ideas and understand their connections. Read the sample paragraph below. Then revise it so that the facts and details are in the most logical order.

> In the mid-1700's, some scientists sent measurement devices higher and higher. Before long, hot-air balloons offered new ways to transport the tools into the sky. At first they used kites.

Word Wise

When you revise, check that sentences are clear and the ideas are easy to follow. You may need to rearrange ideas. For example, *She saw stars looking out the window.* This sentence structure makes it seem like the stars are looking out the window. *Looking out the window, she saw stars* makes more sense.

Revision Revise your draft. Check that you present your facts and specific details in a logical order. Think about what is the best order to help your readers learn about the history and importance of your scientific advancement. Make sure your information correctly tells what you found in your research.

Peer Conferences

Review a Draft Listen carefully as a partner reads his or her work aloud. Take notes about what you liked and what was difficult to follow. Begin by telling what you liked about the draft. Ask questions that will help the writer think more about the writing. Make suggestions that you think will make the writing stronger. Use these sentence starters.

I enjoyed this part of your draft because . . .

That detail does not seem relevant. Can you explain why . . .

I am not sure about the order of . . .

Partner Feedback After your partner gives you feedback on your draft, write one of the suggestions that you will use in your revision. Refer to the rubric on page 31 as you give feedback.

Based on my partner's feedback, I will ______________________________

____

After you finish giving each other feedback, reflect on the peer conference. What was helpful? What might you do differently next time?

Revision As you revise your draft, use the Revising Checklist to help you figure out what ideas you may need to add, delete, combine, or rearrange. Remember to use the rubric on page 31 to help you with your revision.

Digital Tools

For more information about peer conferences, watch the "Peer Conferencing" video. Go to **my.mheducation.com.**

Revising Checklist

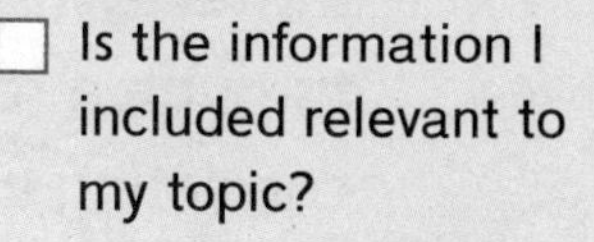

- ☐ Does my writing fit my purpose and audience?
- ☐ Is the information I included relevant to my topic?
- ☐ Do I include facts and specific details that support the main idea?
- ☐ Are my facts and details presented in a logical order?

Edit and Proofread

When you **edit** and **proofread** your writing, you look for and correct mistakes in spelling, punctuation, capitalization, and grammar. Reading through a revised draft multiple times can help you make sure you're correcting any errors. Use the checklist below to edit your sentences.

Editing Checklist

- ☐ Do all sentences begin with a capital letter and end with a punctuation mark?
- ☐ Are there any run-on sentences or sentence fragments?
- ☐ Do all sentences have subject-verb agreement?
- ☐ Are clauses, appositives, and quotes punctuated correctly?
- ☐ Are proper nouns and abbreviations, initials, and acronyms capitalized correctly?
- ☐ Are referenced titles italicized or underlined?
- ☐ Are all words spelled correctly?

List two mistakes you found as you proofread your research report.

1. ____

____

2. ____

____

Tech Tip

Spell checkers are useful tools in word-processing programs, but they may not recognize incorrect words. For example, if you meant to use *we'll,* but typed *well* instead, the spell checker might not catch it. That is why it's important also to do a careful reading.

Grammar Connections

When you proofread your report, make sure that you have capitalized proper nouns, such as names, places, organizations, and events, if they have a specific title or name.

Publish, Present, and Evaluate

Publishing When you publish your writing, you create a clean, neat final copy that is free of mistakes. As you write, be sure to write legibly in cursive. Be sure that you are holding your pencil or pen correctly. Adding visuals can make your writing more interesting for your audience. Consider including illustrations, graphs, or photos to help make your research report more interesting.

Presentation When you are ready to present your work, rehearse your presentation. Use the Presenting Checklist to help you.

Evaluate After you publish your writing, use the rubric below to **evaluate** your writing.

What did you do successfully? ______________________________

What needs more work? ______________________________

____

Presenting Checklist

- ☐ Look at the audience.
- ☐ Speak clearly and slowly.
- ☐ Speak loud enough so that everyone can hear you.
- ☐ Display any visuals so that everyone can see them.
- ☐ Answer questions thoughtfully, using details from your topic.

4	3	2	1
• introduces the topic in a way that captures readers' attention and clearly states the purpose of the report • provides researched facts, specific details, examples, and explanations relevant to the topic • presents information in a logical order	• clearly introduces the topic and purpose of the report • some researched facts, specific details, examples, and explanations are not relevant to the topic • presents information in a mostly logical order	• names the topic, but does not state a purpose of the report • very few facts, specific details, examples, or explanations provided from research • makes an effort to present information in a logical order	• topic or purpose is not clearly stated • does not use facts, specific details, examples, or explanations from research • information is not presented in a logical order

Talk About It

Essential Question

How do shared experiences help people adapt to change?

During the 1930s, people throughout the world experienced the Great Depression. Many people in the United States lost their jobs. They stood in long lines to wait for work. They relied on the kindness of supportive groups, such as the one in the photo. As they waited, people shared stories.

Talk with a partner about how you have adapted to change. What words and phrases come to mind? Write them in the web.

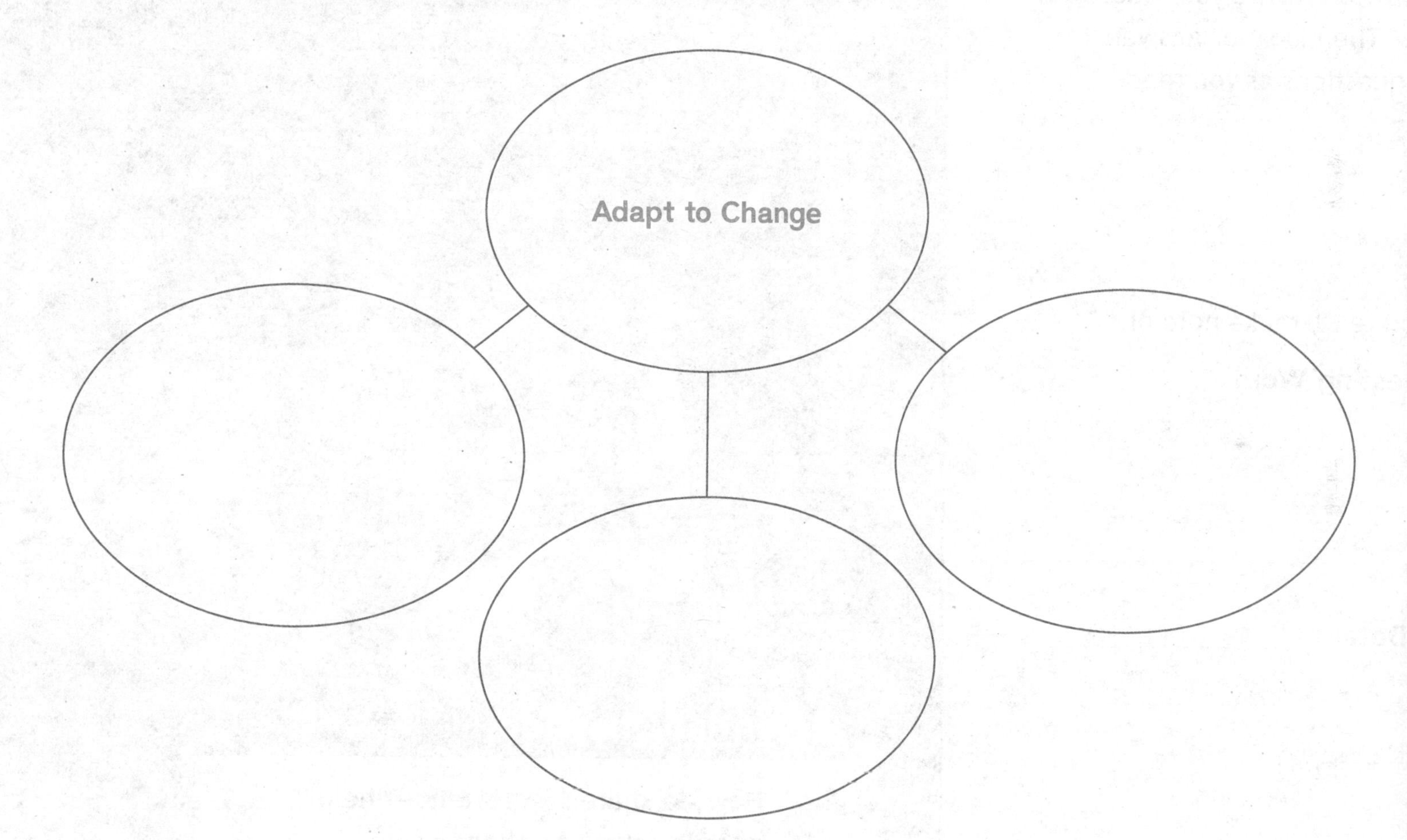

Go online to **my.mheducation.com** and read the "Shared Experiences Through Music" Blast. Think about how shared experiences help people adapt to change. How might music help people come together during times of change? Then blast back your response.

SHARED READ

TAKE NOTES

Before you read, preview the story. Ask questions about the title and illustrations. Write your questions below. Then look for answers to your questions as you read.

____

____

____

As you read, make note of:

Interesting Words ______________

____

____

____

Key Details ______________

____

____

____

____

____

____

The Day the Rollets Got Their Moxie Back

Essential Question

How do shared experiences help people adapt to change?

Read about how a family comes together during a period of great hardship in the United States.

Ron Mazellan

Sometimes, the thing that gets you through hard times comes like a bolt from the blue. That's what my older brother's letter was like, traveling across the country from a work camp in Wyoming. It was 1937, and Ricky was helping to build facilities for a new state park as part of President Roosevelt's employment program. Though the program created jobs for young men like Ricky, it hadn't helped our dad find work yet.

I imagined Ricky looking up at snow-capped mountains and sparkling skies, breathing in the smell of evergreens as his work crew turned trees into lumber and lumber into buildings. It almost made an 11-year-old **weakling** like me want to become a lumberjack.

Back in our New York City apartment, the air smelled like meatloaf and cabbage. Dad sat slant-wise in his chair by the window, **obviously** trying to catch the last rays of sunlight rather than turn on a light. My older sister Ruth and I lay on the floor comparing the letters Ricky had sent us.

"Shirley, Ricky says they had a talent show, and he wore a grass skirt and did a hula dance while playing the ukulele!" Ruth reported with delight. "I'll bet he was the cat's pajamas!"

"It'd be swell to have our own talent show!" I replied.

"Should I start sewing grass skirts?" Mom asked from the kitchen, which was just the corner where someone had plopped down a stove next to a sink and an icebox. "Now come set the table. Dinner's almost ready."

HISTORICAL FICTION

FIND TEXT EVIDENCE

Read

Paragraphs 1–6

Make Predictions

Make a prediction based on the girls' conversation. Write the text evidence for your prediction.

____

____

____

____

Paragraphs 4–5

Dialect

What does the word *swell* mean? **Circle** the context clues in the previous paragraph. Write its meaning here.

____

Reread

Author's Craft

What point of view is the story written from? Why might the author have written the story from this point of view?

SHARED READ

FIND TEXT EVIDENCE

Read

Paragraphs 1–3

Compare and Contrast

Compare and contrast the characters' attitudes at the dinner table. **Circle** words and phrases you used as clues. What are their attitudes?

____

____

____

Paragraph 4

Idioms

What clues in the text help you to understand the meaning of "grin and bear it"?

____

____

Reread

Author's Craft

What message is the author sending by showing how the family responds to their troubles?

Dad stayed where he was, sullen and spent. "Any jobs in the paper?" Mom asked, her voice rich with **sympathy**. Dad shook his head no. He had worked as an artist in the theater for years, but most productions were still strapped for cash. Dad sketched posters for shows that did get the green light, just to keep his skills sharp. He even designed posters for "Rollet's Follies," with Ruth and me depicted in watercolor costumes.

For dinner, Mom served a baked loaf of whatever ingredients she had that worked well together. From the reddish color, I could **assume** that she had snuck in beets. "I **guarantee** you'll like these beets," she said, reading my frown. "It's beet loaf, the meatless meat loaf," she sang as she served up slices.

Ruth fidgeted in her seat, still excited about the talent show. Though calm on the outside, inside I was all atwitter, too.

Over the next week, Ruth and I practiced our Hawaiian dance routine. Our parents worried about heating bills as cold weather settled in. One Saturday, my father decided to grin and bear it, and grab some hot coffee at the local soup kitchen, where he hoped to hear about available jobs. Ruth and I begged to go along. Since the kitchen offered doughnuts and hot chocolate on weekends, he agreed.

Ron Mazellan

Most everyone in line was bundled up against the cold. Many of us had to **rely** on two or three threadbare layers. Like many other men, Dad bowed his head as if in shame.

The line moved slowly. Bored, Ruth began practicing her dance steps. I sang an upbeat tune to give her some music. Around us, downturned hats lifted to reveal frowns becoming smiles. Soon, folks began clapping along. Egged on by the **supportive** response, Ruth twirled and swayed like there was no tomorrow.

"Those girls sure have moxie!" someone shouted.

"They've got heart, all right!" offered another. "Why, they oughta be in pictures!"

"With performances like that, I'd **nominate** them for an Academy Award!" a woman called out.

"Those are my girls!" Dad declared, his head held high.

Everyone burst into applause. For those short moments, the past didn't matter, and the future blossomed ahead of us like a beautiful flower. I couldn't wait to write Ricky and tell him the news.

Summarize

Use your notes to orally summarize the story. Describe each character in your summary.

HISTORICAL FICTION

FIND TEXT EVIDENCE

Read

Paragraphs 1–2

Compare and Contrast

Underline the words that show how the people's mood changes.

Paragraphs 3-7

Confirm Predictions

How accurate was your prediction?

____

____

____

Reread

Author's Craft

How does the author use imagery to show the father has changed by the end of the story?

Fluency

Take turns with a partner reading aloud the first two paragraphs. Read the paragraphs with an appropriate rate.

Vocabulary

Use the example sentences to talk with a partner about each word. Then answer the questions.

assume

Caitlyn could only **assume** the cat had broken the flowerpot since Pip was standing over the pieces.

What might you assume if you awaken to a major snowstorm on a school day?

guarantee

The weather forecaster can **guarantee** that it will rain soon because of the dark clouds approaching.

When else might you guarantee something?

nominate

The team will **nominate** the best candidate for team captain.

When might you nominate a particular person for a task or position?

obviously

The scarf was **obviously** too long for Marta.

What clothes are obviously wrong for a cold day?

rely

Calvin must **rely** on his notes in order to study.

When have you had to rely on someone else?

Build Your Word List Circle the word *supportive* on page 37. In your writer's notebook, list its root word and related words. Then do the same with another word that uses the suffix *-ive*. Use an online or print dictionary to find more related words.

supportive

The audience's **supportive** applause boosted Clare's energy as she played her violin.

How else can you be supportive of a performer on stage?

sympathy

Jamar's dad gave him **sympathy** when his team lost the game.

When else might you express sympathy to someone?

weakling

Being sick in bed made Emily feel like a **weakling**.

Why might being sick make someone feel like a weakling?

Idioms

An **idiom** is an expression that uses words in a creative way. Surrounding words and sentences can help you understand the meaning of an idiom.

FIND TEXT EVIDENCE

I'm not sure what the idiom a bolt from the blue *means on page 35. When I think of a "bolt," I think of lightning and how quickly and unpredictably it can strike. Letters often come unexpectedly, as if out of nowhere. That must be the meaning.*

Sometimes, the thing that gets you through hard times comes like a bolt from the blue. That's what my older brother's letter was like, traveling across the country from a work camp in Wyoming.

Your Turn Use context clues to explain the meanings of the following idioms from "The Day the Rollets Got Their Moxie Back."

the cat's pajamas, *page 35*

get the green light, *page 36*

Make Predictions

Making predictions helps you read with purpose. As you read a story, illustrations and clues in the text can help you predict what will happen next. Understanding the characteristics of a genre can also help inform your prediction. As you continue to read, you can confirm if your predictions are correct.

Quick Tip

Think about what is happening in the story. Pay attention to what the characters are doing. This will help you think about what might happen next. Don't forget to check your prediction as you continue to read.

FIND TEXT EVIDENCE

You can make predictions about the story "The Day the Rollets Got Their Moxie Back," beginning with the genre label and the title.

Page 34

From the title, I predict that the main characters in the historical fiction story will be the Rollets. The story will probably have a positive ending since the Rollets will get back something that they have been missing.

Your Turn Use the illustration and the last paragraph on page 36 to discuss a prediction readers might make about the story.

Dialect

"The Day the Rollets Got Their Moxie Back" is historical fiction. It features events and settings typical of the time in which the story takes place. The author uses dialect, a kind of literary device, to show characters who act and speak like the people from a particular place in the past.

FIND TEXT EVIDENCE

I can tell that "The Day the Rollets Got Their Moxie Back" is historical fiction. The year is 1937, and President Roosevelt was real. Rollet family members use dialect of the time, which contributes to the story's voice.

Readers to Writers

Dialect is not only associated with history, but is also related to certain places. For example, people from the West might have different sayings from those in the South. Are there any sayings specific to where you live?

Page 35

Sometimes, the thing that gets you through hard times comes like a bolt from the blue. That's what my older brother's letter was like, traveling across the country from a work camp in Wyoming. It was 1937, and Ricky was helping to build facilities for a new state park as part of President Roosevelt's employment program. Though the program created jobs for young men like Ricky, it hadn't helped our dad find work yet.

I imagined Ricky looking up at snow-capped mountains and sparkling skies, breathing in the smell of evergreens as his work crew turned trees into lumber and lumber into buildings. It almost made an 11-year-old **weakling** like me want to become a lumberjack.

Back in our New York City apartment, the air smelled like meatloaf and cabbage. Dad sat slant-wise in his chair by the window, **obviously** trying to catch the last rays of sunlight rather than turn on a light. My older sister Ruth and I lay on the floor comparing the letters Ricky had sent us.

"Shirley, Ricky says they had a talent show, and he wore a grass skirt and did a hula dance while playing the ukulele!" Ruth reported with delight. "I'll bet he was the cat's pajamas!"

"It'd be swell to have our own talent show!" I replied.

"Should I start sewing grass skirts?" Mom asked from the kitchen, which was just the corner where someone had plopped down a stove next to a sink and an icebox. "Now come set the table. Dinner's almost ready."

Dialect

Characters sometimes use dialect, which is speech typical of a place or time. Dialect may include words, phrases, and idioms that might sound unfamiliar.

Your Turn List another example of dialect in "The Day the Rollets Got Their Moxie Back." Why might an author include dialect in historical fiction?

____

____

____

____

Compare and Contrast

The characters in a story may be similar to or different from one another in their traits, actions, and responses to events. You **compare and contrast** characters to help you better understand how their personalities and actions affect events or are changed by events. This helps you analyze characters' relationships and the conflicts, or problems, they have.

Quick Tip

The following words and phrases are clues to comparing and contrasting.

Compare: *same as, like, similar, alike*

Contrast: *different, not the same, unlike*

FIND TEXT EVIDENCE

When I reread page 35 of "The Day the Rollets Got Their Moxie Back," I can use text details to compare the family members' actions before dinner.

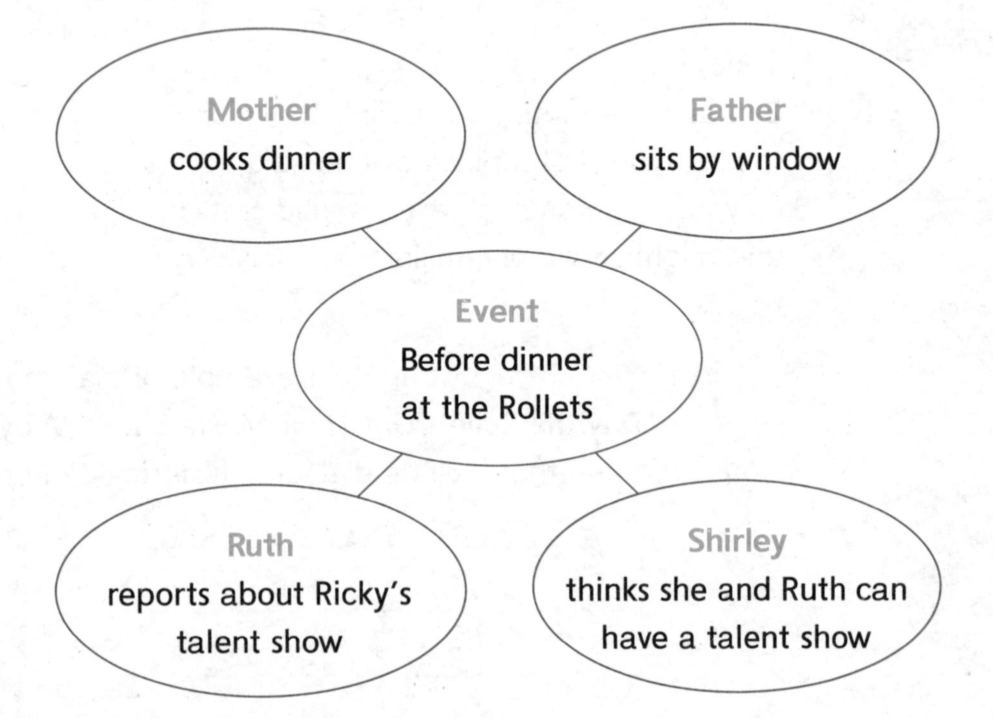

Your Turn Compare the characters' actions at the soup kitchen. Complete the graphic organizer on page 43.

Ron Mazellan

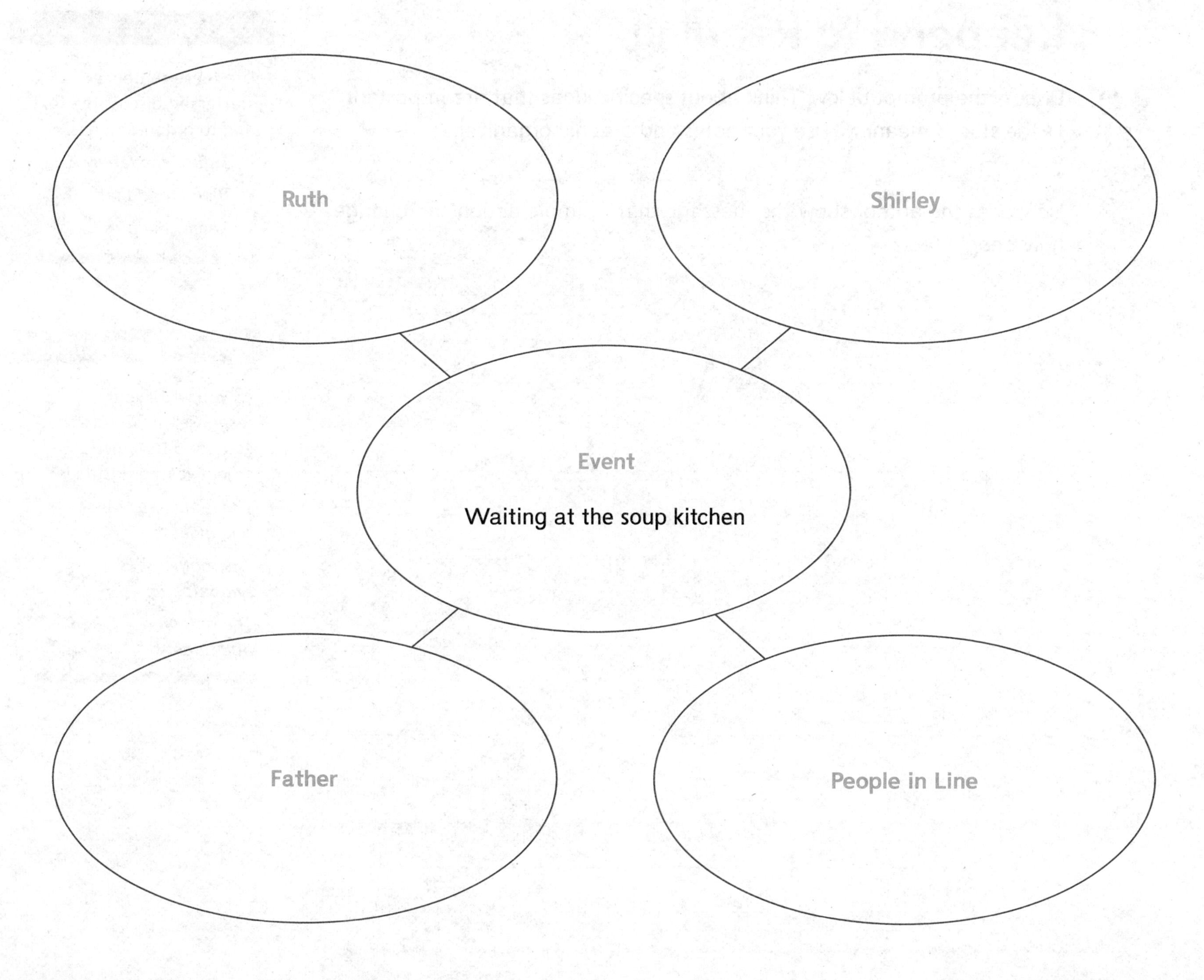
Ruth
Shirley
Event
Waiting at the soup kitchen
Father
People in Line

Respond to Reading

Discuss the prompt below. Think about specific ideas that are important to the story's meaning. Use your notes and graphic organizer.

How does the author show the message that a simple action can change how people feel?

Quick Tip

Use these sentence starters to discuss the text and to organize ideas.

- *At first, the family is. . .*
- *Then I read that. . .*
- *Finally, the girls. . .*

Grammar Connections

As you write your response, make sure that you use descriptive adjectives. For instance:

*The father was **sullen** and **quiet**.*

*The mother was **sympathetic**.*

*The girls were **excited** and **fidgety**.*

Credible Sources

A **credible primary source** or **secondary source** has information that can be trusted. Print and online resources may contain primary and secondary sources. When using online resources, ask yourself:

- Is the source identified and well known for accuracy?
- Is the information in the source well-organized?
- Is information documented and credited?

What else can you do to check if an online source is credible?

____

____

A library is a good place to find credible sources. Librarians can help you follow your research plan by suggesting good texts.

Create a Collage With a partner or in a group, create a collage about the Great Depression. A collage is a work of art that combines different materials, images, and text to show a topic or an idea. Think about these ideas to help focus your topic:

- leaders who tried to solve the problems people had
- different struggles that farmers and people in the cities faced
- resources and entertainment that helped people have some fun

Discuss what credible sources you might use in your research. You may find what you need in books, magazines, and online. Don't forget to ask an adult to help you follow your research plan.

Tech Tip

Ask your teacher or another adult to recommend collage-maker programs you can use. Many programs will allow you to shape your collage and add text, labels, and backgrounds as well as photos and art.

Reread | ANCHOR TEXT

Literature Anthology: pages 366–379

Bud, Not Buddy

What does the author reveal about Bud through his responses to the conversation he overhears?

Talk About It Reread **Literature Anthology** pages 368–369. Discuss with your partner what Bud thinks and does. Discuss why he reacts in this way.

Cite Text Evidence What does Bud do after he overhears the conversation? Write text evidence in the chart.

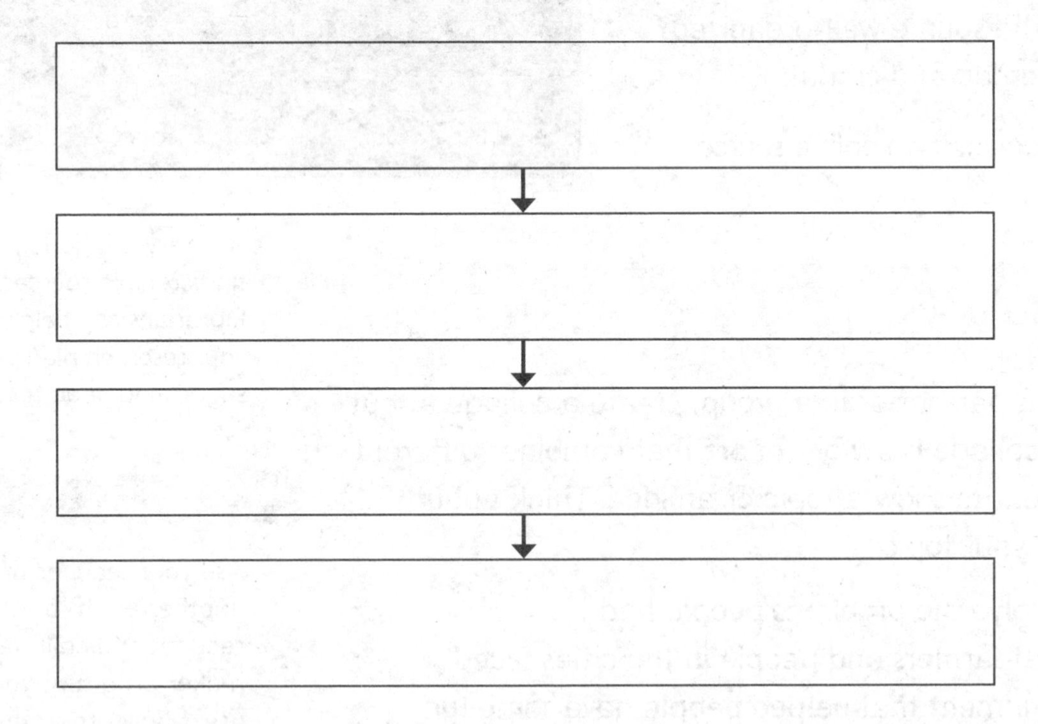

Write The author helps me know more about Bud by ______

______

______

Evaluate Information

Looking at what a character says and does can help you evaluate the character's behavior and analyze his or her relationship with other characters. Evaluate the things Bud does after he overhears the conversation. How does this help you understand how the author wants readers to feel about Bud?

How does the author show how Bud will have to change to stay with the band?

Talk About It Reread **Literature Anthology** page 372. Turn to your partner and discuss what Bud is expected to do. Discuss specific ideas in the text that are important to the meaning.

Cite Text Evidence How is what Bud is expected to do different from what he is used to? Write text evidence in the chart.

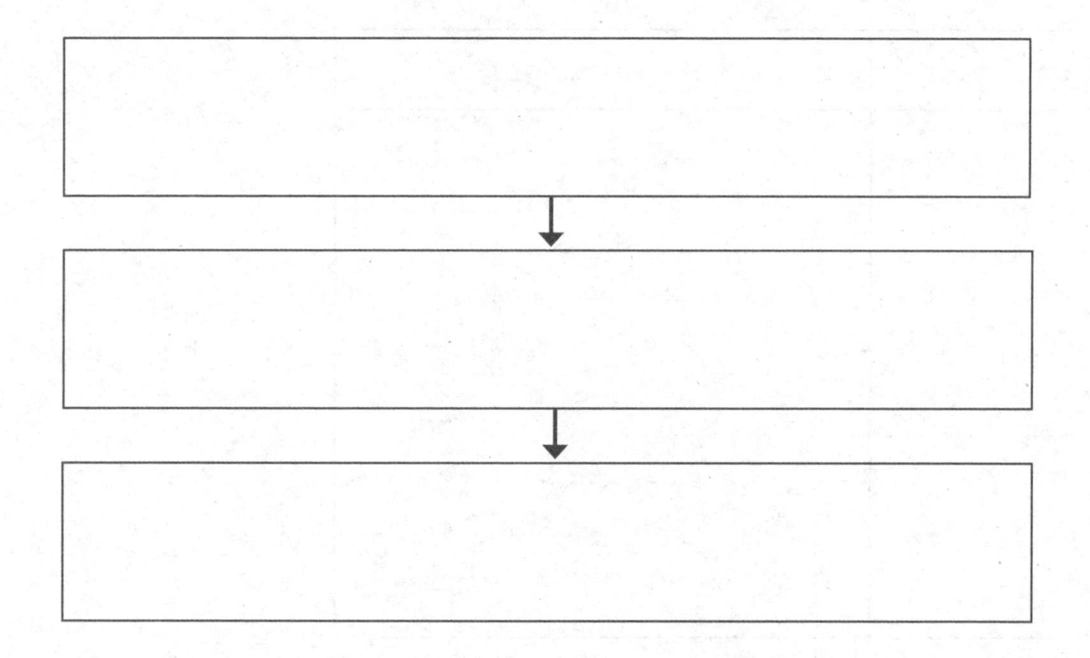

Write The author helps me understand how Bud will have to change by

Quick Tip

Think about where Bud is now and the people he spends his time with. What is Bud learning about them?

Make Inferences

Recalling earlier details in a story can help you make inferences. Think about what you know of the band. Why is it significant that Steady Eddie gives Bud his old alto saxophone case?

Reread | ANCHOR TEXT

How does the author help you understand how Bud changes as he becomes part of the band?

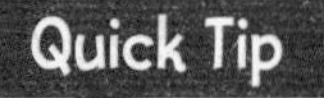

Quick Tip

Rereading can help you think about why characters act a certain way. How does Bud act when he hears his new name?

Talk About It Reread **Literature Anthology** page 378. Turn to a partner and discuss how Bud feels about his new nickname and what he is expected to do. Evaluate details in the story to determine key ideas.

Cite Text Evidence What words and phrases help you see how Bud changes? Write text evidence.

Text Evidence	How It Helps

Write I understand how Bud changes because the author ______________________

____

____

____

Respond to Reading

Discuss the prompt below. Apply your own knowledge about why rules might need to change. Use your notes and graphic organizer.

How does the author show how the significance of Bud's set of rules changes and plays a role in the message of the story?

Quick Tip

Use these sentence starters to talk about and cite text evidence.

- *The rules change. . .*
- *This is important because. . .*
- *This affects the story. . .*

Self-Selected Reading

Choose a text and fill in your writer's notebook with the title, author, and genre. Record your purpose for reading. For example, you may be reading to answer a question or for entertainment.

Photo Spin/Getty Images

Reread | PAIRED SELECTION

Literature Anthology: pages 382–385

Musical Impressions of the Great Depression

Sympathy through Song

1 Many songs of the 1930s, particularly in folk and country music, recounted people's stories of loss and hardship. The songwriter Woody Guthrie followed farm workers who traveled west to California hoping to find work. He saw that they often encountered new and tougher challenges. Guthrie expressed sympathy for them through songs like "Dust Bowl Blues" and "Goin' Down the Road Feeling Bad." He hoped to restore people's sense of dignity.

2 Meanwhile, across the country, the Carter Family performed similar songs, such as "Worried Man Blues," describing life in the Appalachian Mountains where resources were scarce. Listeners found comfort in the knowledge that they were not alone in their struggles.

Reread the excerpt. Evaluate details to determine key ideas. **Underline** the sentence that explains the goal of Woody Guthrie's music. Write how this kind of music affected people who struggled during this time.

____

____

____

____

____

Talk with your partner about why music was able to change how people felt during a difficult time. **Circle** text evidence in the excerpt.

On the Up-Swing

3 Times were certainly hard in the country. In the nation's cities, the situation was equally difficult. In some African-American communities, unemployment soared above fifty percent. These challenges reminded some of earlier times of slavery, and many found comfort in the musical styles of that era: gospel and blues.

4 Jazz, a newer form of music with upbeat rhythms, lifted people's spirits. Band leaders like Duke Ellington and Count Basie created a new, high-energy style of jazz called swing. Around the country, people of all races responded to these positive rhythms. People left their problems behind and escaped onto the dance floor.

5 In New York, Broadway musicals delighted theatergoers. Many musicals offered light entertainment, while others addressed the current hardships through songs, such as "Brother, Can You Spare a Dime?" Radio helped spread these songs beyond the city, connecting people across the country and creating nationwide hits.

Reread paragraphs 3 and 4. **Circle** examples of music that affected people.

With a partner, talk about how the author describes the different kinds of music. **Underline** a sentence in paragraph 5 that describes another kind of music that affected people.

Why is "On the Up-Swing" a good heading for this section? Evaluate details and use text evidence to support your answer.

Reread | PAIRED SELECTION

What is the author's purpose for writing this selection?

Talk About It Reread the excerpts on pages 50 and 51. Discuss what the author wants you to know about music during the Great Depression.

Cite Text Evidence What words and phrases tell you why the author wrote this selection? Write text evidence in the chart.

Clues	Author's Purpose

Write The author's purpose for writing this selection was ______________________________

____

____

____

____

____

Quick Tip

When you reread, pay close attention to the details the author provides. Evaluating the details the author provides helps you understand if the author's purpose is to entertain, inform, or persuade the reader.

Text Structure

When authors use a compare-and-contrast text structure, they show how ideas can be alike and different while supporting a central idea. Authors use signal words and phrases, such as *however, while,* or *similarly*.

FIND TEXT EVIDENCE

On page 51 in paragraph 5, the author compares and contrasts how Broadway musicals helped people through hard times. The word *while* is a clue that something is being compared.

> In New York, Broadway musicals delighted theatergoers. Many musicals offered light entertainment, while others addressed the current hardships through songs, such as "Brother, Can You Spare a Dime?"

Your Turn Reread paragraphs 1 and 2 on page 50.

- What is the author comparing and contrasting? ______________________

____

____

____

- What is the central idea of these two paragraphs? ______________________

____

____

Readers to Writers

When you write an informational text, you must have a central, or main, idea. You need to support your central idea with evidence, such as facts. Before writing, you should decide which text structure to use to present your evidence. For example, you may use cause-and-effect, compare-and-contrast, or problem-and-solution.

Text Connections

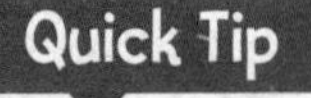

Quick Tip

Look carefully at the photograph. Use clues from the photo and ideas you read about to talk about how music affects people.

How do this photograph and the selections *Bud, Not Buddy* and "Musical Impressions of the Great Depression" demonstrate the effects that music can have on people?

Talk About It Look at the photograph. Read the caption. With a partner, talk about what is going on and how it makes you feel.

Cite Text Evidence **Circle** details in the photograph that help you understand what people are feeling. **Draw a box** around the main focus of the photo.

Write The photograph and selections show ______________________________

____

____

____

____

____

____

____

Portrait of Ella Fitzgerald with Dizzy Gillespie, Ray Brown, and other musicians at the Downbeat Club in New York in 1947.

Present Your Work

Discuss how you will present your collage about the Great Depression, such as describing photos like the one below that shows shacks in a park during the Great Depression. Use the Presenting Checklist as you practice your presentation. Discuss the sentence starters below and write your answers.

New ideas I learned about the Great Depression helped me to understand ______________________________

____

____

I would like to know more about ______________________________

____

____

____

Quick Tip

Plan how you will introduce and describe your collage. State your topic and then briefly explain how you created your collage. Next, point out different parts of your collage and what they represent.

Presenting Checklist

- ☐ Plan with your partner or group who will give each part of your presentation.
- ☐ Have each student rehearse the parts of the presentation.
- ☐ Use an appropriate mode of delivery for your information.
- ☐ Speak slowly, clearly, and with appropriate volume.
- ☐ Make eye contact with your audience.
- ☐ Allow time for questions. Listen carefully and provide complete answers.

Talk About It

Essential Question

How do natural events and human activities affect the environment?

We are surrounded by many species of plants and animals that are not native to the area they live in. Look at the photo. It shows a beekeeper. Beekeeping is not an activity that is only done in the country. This beekeeper keeps honey bees in a busy city. Bees can thrive in this unusual setting and produce honey.

Talk with a partner about activities that affect the environment. Write your ideas in the web about how natural and human activities affect the environment.

SCIENCE

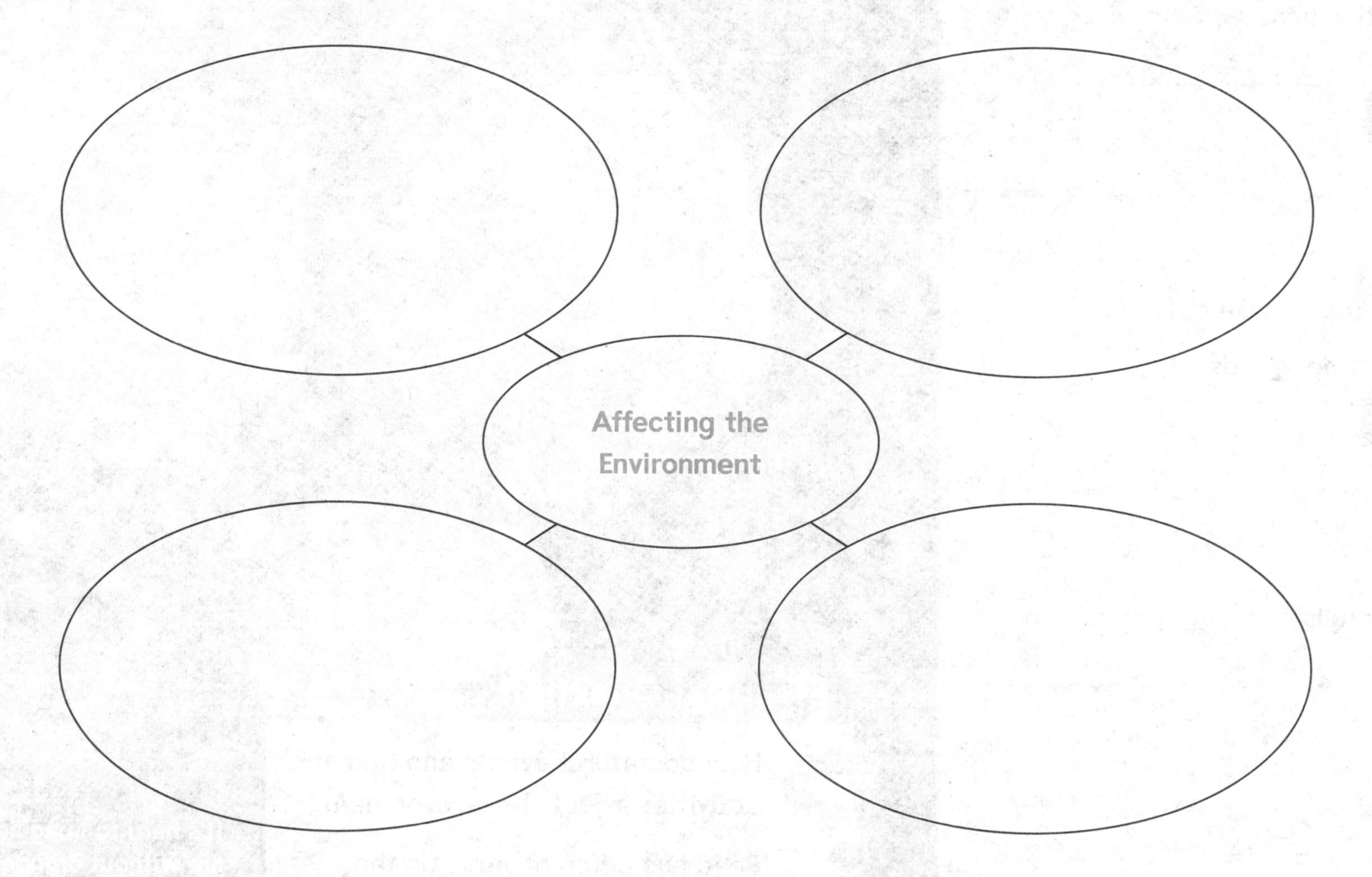

Go online to **my.mheducation.com** and read the "Leaving a Trace" Blast. Think about some ways that human activities might continue to effect the natural world. Then blast back your response.

Adrian Dennis/AFP/Getty Images

SHARED READ

TAKE NOTES

Before you begin reading, preview the title and the subheads. Then make a prediction about what you think you will learn. Write your prediction here.

____

____

____

____

As you read, make note of

Interesting Words ______________

____

____

____

Key Details ______________

____

____

____

____

____

____

Kirk Weddle/Photodisc/Getty Images

Essential Question

How do natural events and human activities affect the environment?

Read two different views on the arrival of new species into the United States.

It's hard to imagine life without oranges and chickens, which are examples of nonnative species.

Should Plants and Animals from Other Places Live Here?

New Arrivals Welcome

Nonnative species are good for the economy—and they taste good, too!

Some of America's important recent inhabitants are plants and animals. Called *nonnative species*, these creatures arrive here from other regions or countries. Nonnative species are known as *invasive* when they harm the environment, our health, or the economy. Invasive species often take over a **widespread** area and overwhelm native wildlife. The population of some native species has **declined** because of a few newcomers, but the news is not all bad. We would be a lot worse off without some of them.

In Florida, for example, about 2,000 species of familiar plants and animals are nonnative. These include oranges, chickens, and sugarcane. In fact, 90 percent of farm sales can be traced directly to nonnative species.

Nonnative species help to control insects and other pests that harm crops. Some scientists **identify** a pest's natural enemy and bring in nonnative enemy species, such as insects, to kill the pests. Killing the pests is a good thing, and an even better result is that pesticide use is reduced. Vedalia beetles were transported here from Australia to eat insects that killed citrus fruit. The beetles completed their mission without any side effects. They also help keep citrus farmers in business!

Not all new arrivals benefit humans. However, many nonnative species are just what the doctor ordered. Many of the dogs and cats we love so much originated in other parts of the world. Would you want to ban Labrador retrievers and Siamese cats? Creatures like these surely make our lives and our nation better!

ARGUMENTATIVE TEXT

FIND TEXT EVIDENCE

Read

Paragraphs 1–2

Author's Point of View

Write the author's claim about nonnative species.

____

____

Underline the details that support this claim.

Paragraphs 3–4

Ask and Answer Questions

Write a question you can ask to check your understanding about the plan to control insects and pests. Circle the answer.

____

____

____

Reread

Author's Craft

Why does the author talk about both invasive nonnative species and helpful nonnative species?

FIND TEXT EVIDENCE

Read

Paragraphs 1–4

Author's Point of View

Write the author's claim about nonnative species.

____

____

Underline specific examples the author gives to support this claim.

Paragraph 5

Root Words

How does the Latin root *clus*, meaning "to shut," help you understand the meaning of *conclusion*?

____

____

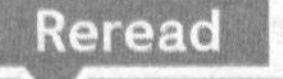

Reread

Author's Craft

How does the author help you understand how invasive species got to this country?

A Growing Problem

Thousands of foreign plant and animal species threaten our country.

Visitors to the Florida Everglades expect to see alligators, not pythons. These huge snakes are native to Southeast Asia. But about 150,000 of the reptiles are crawling through the Everglades. The **probable** reason they got there is that pet owners dumped the snakes in the wild. Now the nonnative pythons have become a **widespread** menace, threatening to reduce the population of endangered native species.

Some nonnative species may be useful, but others are harmful to the nation. It costs the U.S. more than $120 billion each year to repair the damage these species cause to the environment. The trouble occurs when nonnative species become invasive. Invasive species are a nuisance just about everywhere in the nation. For example, the Asian carp, which was introduced unintentionally to the U.S., has been able to **thrive** in the Mississippi River and now threatens the Great Lakes ecosystem. Because of its large appetite, the population of native fish has gone down.

Some germs are also invasive species, and they are especially harmful to humans. One, the avian influenza virus, came to the U.S. carried by birds. This microbe can cause a serious lung **disorder** in infected people.

Some **agricultural** experts have introduced nonnative species on purpose to improve the environment. However, this can sometimes create **unexpected** problems. A hundred years ago, melaleuca trees were brought to Florida from Australia to stabilize swampy areas. Now millions of the trees blanket the land, crowding out native plants and harming endangered plants and animals.

The facts about this alien invasion lead to one conclusion: We must remove invasive species and keep new ones from our shores.

Nonnative Species: Benefits and Costs

Over the years, about 50,000 nonnative species have entered the U.S. These four examples show the positive and negative impacts they can have.

SPECIES	NATIVE LAND	WHEN AND HOW INTRODUCED TO U.S.	POSITIVE IMPACT	NEGATIVE IMPACT
Horse	Europe	Early 1500s, on purpose	Used for work, transportation, and recreation	Made large-scale wars possible
Kudzu	Asia	Early 1800s, on purpose	Stops soil erosion	Crowds out native plants
Olives	Middle East and Europe	Early 1700s, on purpose, cultivation began in 1800s	Major food and cooking oil source, important industry in California	Uses much of the limited supply of water in California
Mediterranean Fruit Fly	Sub-Saharan Africa	1929 (first recorded), accidentally	May be a food source for creatures such as spiders	Destroys 400 species of plants, including citrus and vegetable crops

This community is trying to control the invasive melaleuca plant that has taken over this marsh.

Summarize

Use your notes to write a short summary of the topic and the opposing points of view presented in the selection.

Talk about whether your prediction on page 58 was correct.

ARGUMENTATIVE TEXT

FIND TEXT EVIDENCE

Read

Charts and Headings

Look at the chart. Which species do you think had more of an impact on people than on the environment? Explain your answer.

____

____

____

____

____

Reread

Author's Craft

Why do you think this chart was used to end the selection?

Vocabulary

Use the example sentences to talk with a partner about each word. Then answer the questions.

agricultural

Sam and Gina sell apples and other **agricultural** products at the farmers' market.

How do agricultural products make a difference in your life?

declined

Because many businesses closed, the town had clearly **declined** over the years.

What might happen if a restaurant's profits have declined?

disorder

The veterinarian examined the cow for a stomach **disorder**.

What kind of medical disorder might keep you home from school?

identify

People are able to **identify** my dog by his long ears.

How would you quickly identify your best friend in a crowd?

probable

The **probable** cause of the shattered window was Jack and his soccer ball.

What type of weather is most probable in the winter where you live?

Build Your Word List Pick a word you found interesting in the selection you read. Look up synonyms and antonyms of the word in a print or digital thesaurus and write them in your writer's notebook.

thrive

Some plants manage to grow and **thrive** even in snow.

What would you do to help a pet thrive?

____

____

____

unexpected

Shoveling the snow was hard work, but it was made easier by the **unexpected** help of our neighbors.

What kind of unexpected event would make you change your plans?

____

____

____

widespread

Starlings, introduced from England, are now a **widespread** bird species.

What is a good example of a widespread fad?

____

____

Root Words

A **root word** is the basic word part that gives a word its main meaning. Knowing the meaning of a root is a key to identifying many words that share that root.

FIND TEXT EVIDENCE

In the first paragraph of "New Arrivals Welcome" on page 59, I read the word invasive. *It has the same root as* invade: vas *and* vad *both come from a Latin word meaning "to go." Something invasive goes into areas beyond its boundaries.*

Nonnative species are known as *invasive* when they harm the environment, our health, or the economy.

Your Turn Use the roots below to figure out the meanings of words from "New Arrivals Welcome" and "A Growing Problem." List other words you know that contain those roots.

Roots: *nativus* = to be born *avis* = bird

nonnative, *page 59* ______________________________

avian, *page 60* ______________________________

Matt Meadows/Peter Arnold/Getty Images

Ask and Answer Questions

To check your understanding of an argumentative text, pause at different points and ask yourself questions about what you have read so far. Then look for answers. You can also generate questions about the whole text when you have finished to help deepen your understanding.

FIND TEXT EVIDENCE

After you read the article "New Arrivals Welcome" on page 59, you might ask yourself, *What is the main idea of this article? What is the author claiming?*

Quick Tip

Some questions you can ask yourself include:

- *Why am I reading this text?*
- *What important details are given?*
- *What am I unclear about?*
- *What connections can I make between information in the article and what I already know?*

Page 59

In Florida, for example, about 2,000 species of familiar plants and animals are nonnative. These include oranges, chickens, and sugarcane. In fact, 90 percent of farm sales can be traced directly to nonnative species.

When I reread, I learn to answer my question. The main idea is that many species in the United States are nonnative, but can be very useful to us. Examples such as oranges and sugarcane support this.

Your Turn Ask and answer a question about "A Growing Problem" on page 60. Reread the article as necessary. As you reread, use the strategy Ask and Answer Questions. Write your question and answer.

____

____

____

Charts and Headings

"New Arrivals Welcome" and "A Growing Problem" are argumentative texts. Argumentative text tries to persuade a reader to support a claim, or viewpoint. The author makes a claim and uses facts for or against an argument. Argumentive text may include text features, such as charts and headings.

FIND TEXT EVIDENCE

Both selections reveal the authors' viewpoints about nonnative species. Facts and evidence support their opinions. A chart has headings and information for comparing the two points of view.

Readers to Writers

When writers write to persuade, they need to give information that is easy to read and understand. Many writers include charts. Charts are a good way to give information in an easy-to-read format. How could you use a chart in your own writing to achieve your purposes?

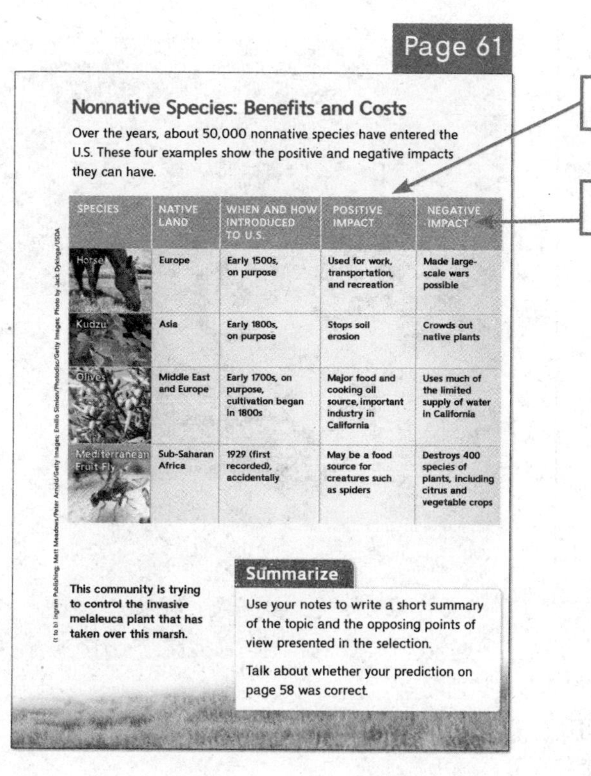

Page 61

Nonnative Species: Benefits and Costs

Over the years, about 50,000 nonnative species have entered the U.S. These four examples show the positive and negative impacts they can have.

SPECIES	NATIVE LAND	WHEN AND HOW INTRODUCED TO U.S.	POSITIVE IMPACT	NEGATIVE IMPACT
Horse	Europe	Early 1500s, on purpose	Used for work, transportation, and recreation	Made large-scale wars possible
Kudzu	Asia	Early 1800s, on purpose	Stops soil erosion	Crowds out native plants
Olives	Middle East and Europe	Early 1700s, on purpose, cultivation began in 1800s	Major food and cooking oil source, important industry in California	Uses much of the limited supply of water in California
Mediterranean Fruit Fly	Sub-Saharan Africa	1929 (first recorded), accidentally	May be a food source for creatures such as spiders	Destroys 400 species of plants, including citrus and vegetable crops

(t to b) Ingram Publishing; Matt Meadows/Peter Arnold/Getty Images; Emilio Simion/Photodisc/Getty Images; Photo by Jack Dykinga/USDA

This community is trying to control the invasive melaleuca plant that has taken over this marsh.

Summarize

Use your notes to write a short summary of the topic and the opposing points of view presented in the selection.

Talk about whether your prediction on page 58 was correct.

Chart

A chart organizes information so it can be analyzed.

Headings

Headings identify the main categories of information.

Your Turn Analyze the information in the chart on page 61. Identify a species that has a mostly positive impact and one that has a mostly negative impact. Explain your conclusions.

Author's Point of View

In an argumentative text, the **author's point of view,** or claim, is the author's position on a topic. To find an author's point of view, look at the author's choice of words, reasons, and factual evidence used to explain the argument for or against an idea.

Quick Tip

Words that describe things in a negative or positive way can give you clues to the author's point of view.

FIND TEXT EVIDENCE

I see from the title "A Growing Problem" on page 60 that the author might have a negative point of view toward nonnative species. The word threaten *expresses a negative emotion, and the facts about pythons support a negative viewpoint.*

Details	Author's Point of View
"A Growing Problem"	The author opposes nonnative species because many become invasive, or hurt native species.
"threaten our country"	
150,000 pythons a "menace"	
Asian carp eat native fish	
"crowding out native plants"	

Photo by Jack Dykinga/USDA

Your Turn Identify important details in "New Arrivals Welcome" and write them in your graphic organizer on page 67. Then identify the author's point of view.

Details

→

Author's Point of View

Respond to Reading

Discuss the prompt below. Think about how each argumentative text is organized and the information presented. Use your notes and graphic organizer.

Did you find one author's argument more convincing than the other? Explain your answer.

Quick Tip

Use these sentence starters to discuss the text and to organize text evidence.

- *I found the argument more convincing because . . .*
- *The author points out that . . .*
- *The author gives examples . . .*

Grammar Connections

As you write your response, you can use comparative forms to talk about the two different arguments. When you compare two ideas, use *more, less, better* and *worse*. For more than two ideas, use *most, least, best,* and *worst*.

SCIENCE

A Research Plan

Developing a **research plan** for a project will help you focus on getting the information you need. The type of research you do will depend on what you want your final product to be. Here are some questions you should ask yourself as you create a research plan:

- What is my project about?
- Where can I find information?
- How am I presenting the information? Is it a poster, a performance, a written report, a blog report, or another format?
- Would including photos, videos, or sounds help to show my information?

What are additional types of information you could present?

____

____

COLLABORATE

Create a Mock Blog Report With a partner or in a group, create a written blog report on a nonnative species, including predicting its effect on the ecosystem. Decide what types of information you will include. Use the following questions to help you choose:

- What does the animal or plant species look like? Would a video link or photo put into the blog work best?
- Are there sounds or other recordings I want to include?
- Do I want to include links to other websites?

After you complete your blog report, you will present it to your class. Discuss the most effective modes, or ways, to present your information.

Starlings are invasive birds that travel in huge flocks. They steal food from other animals as they forage.

In addition to photos, what audio and/or visual might you use in a blog about invasive starlings?

____

____

____

____

Reread | ANCHOR TEXT

The Case of the Missing Bees

Literature Anthology: pages 386–389

Why does the author begin the selection with a question?

COLLABORATE

Talk About It Reread the first paragraph on **Literature Anthology** page 387. Talk with a partner about what the question helps you understand about bees.

Cite Text Evidence How does the author organize the first paragraph? Write text evidence in the chart.

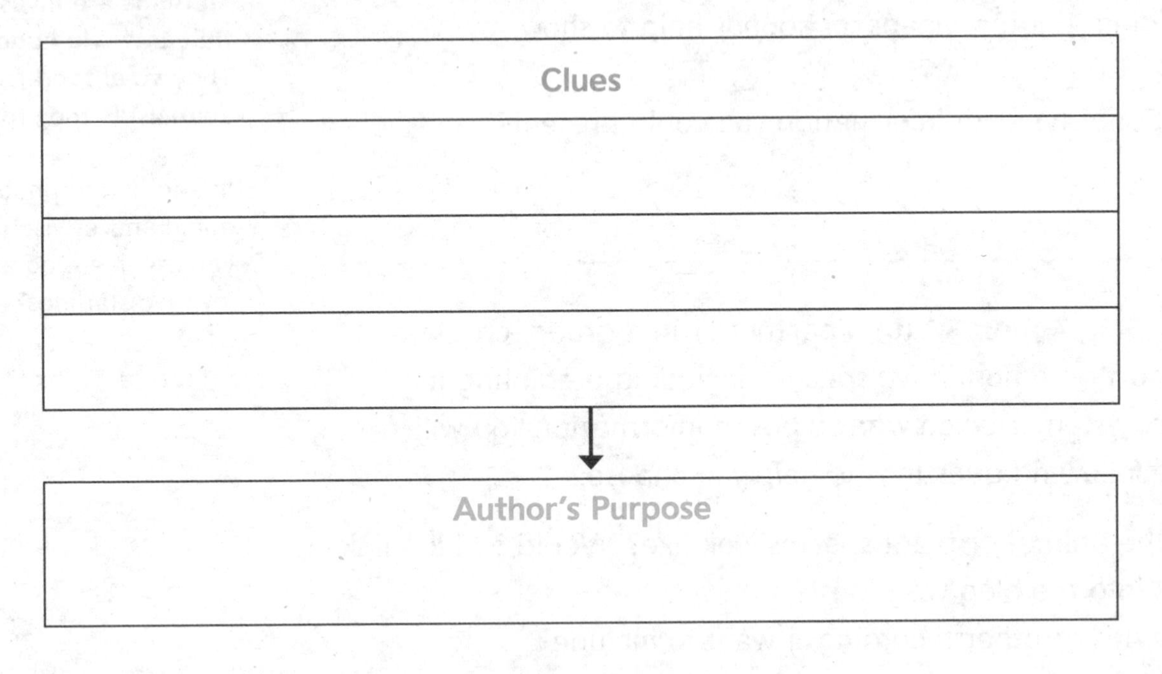

Write The author begins the article with a question to ______________________

____

____

Make Inferences

Reread the question at the beginning of the paragraph. Can you answer it? Is the subject of the question interesting? What inference can you make about why the author includes the question based on your answers?

How does the author's use of headings help you understand his or her point of view about pesticides?

Talk About It Look at the headings on **Literature Anthology** pages 388-389. Turn to a partner and discuss how the headings help the author tell how he or she feels about pesticides.

Cite Text Evidence What words and phrases support the author's headings? Write text evidence and tell how it shows the author's point of view.

The Unusual Suspects	Are Pesticides to Blame?	Author's Point of View

Write The author uses headings to ______________________________

____

____

____

____

Quick Tip

Headings in a chart identify the main categories of information. As you read, think about how the headings in the article have a similar purpose.

Respond to Reading

Discuss the prompt below. Reread the articles if necessary and use your notes and graphic organizer to inform your answer.

Think about how each argumentative article is organized. Which author's style is more convincing and why?

Quick Tip

Use these sentence starters to talk about and cite text evidence.

- *The author of "A Germ of an Idea" thinks . . .*
- *The author of "Pointing to Pesticides" believes . . .*
- *The way the authors organize information helps me see that . . .*

Self-Selected Reading

Choose a text and fill in your writer's notebook with the title, author, and genre. Include a personal response to the text in your writer's notebook.

Reread | PAIRED SELECTION

Busy, Beneficial Bees

1 In the U.S., honeybees pollinate about $15 billion worth of crops a year. That's on top of the $150 million worth of honey they produce annually. Although some crops can be pollinated by other nectar-feeding insects, many crops depend specifically on honeybees for pollination. Without honeybees, our crops and our economy would really feel the sting!

Crops Depend on Honeybees

Many crops depend on insects to pollinate them. For some crops, honeybees make up a large percentage of those pollinators.

Crop	Dependence on Insect Pollination	Proportion that are Honeybees
Alfalfa, hay & seed	100%	60%
Apples	100%	90%
Almonds	100%	100%
Citrus	20-80%	10-90%
Cotton	20%	90%
Soybeans	10%	50%
Broccoli	100%	90%
Carrots	100%	90%
Cantaloupe	80%	90%

Numbers based on estimates in 2000. Source: Compiled by CRS using values reported in R. A. Morse, and N.W. Calderone, *The Value of Honey Bees as Pollinators of U.S. Crops in 2000,* March 2000, Cornell University.

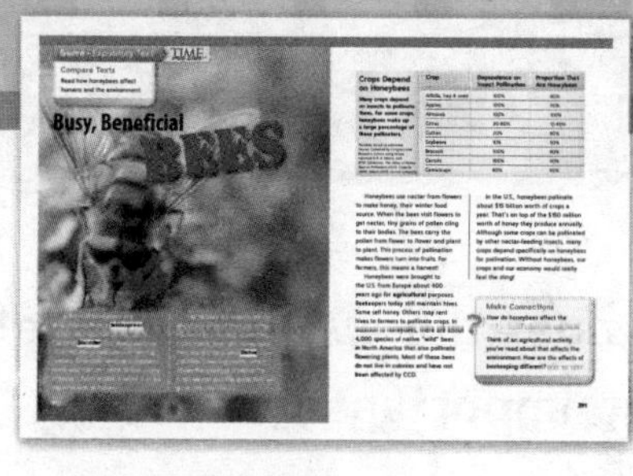

Literature Anthology: pages 390-391

Reread paragraph 1. **Underline** how the author feels about honeybees. Write it here:

____

____

____

____

Reread the section "Crops Depend on Honeybees." Talk with a partner about why the author includes the chart in this selection. **Circle** text evidence to support your discussion.

Make marks in the table beside the top four crops that depend on insect and honeybee pollination.

Reread | PAIRED SELECTION

How does the author use a table to help you understand why bees are so important?

Talk About It Reread the table on page 73. With a partner, discuss how it helps support the author's point of view about honeybees.

Cite Text Evidence What information in the table helps support the author's point of view about the importance of bees? Write text evidence in the chart.

Evidence	Author's Purpose

Write I understand why bees are so important because the author uses a table to ______________________________

____

____

____

Quick Tip

When you read the table, look at the headings for each column first (top row). Then read the information in each row, comparing the second and third columns.

Photo by Stephen Ausmus - USDA-ARS

Word Choice

Puns are words or phrases used in a funny way that suggest a different meaning. Puns sometimes are called "a play on words." Writers may use puns to make a joke so readers will laugh. But the pun may also contain a message for readers.

FIND TEXT EVIDENCE

In "Busy, Beneficial Bees," the author ends the paragraph about honeybees with a pun.

> Without honeybees, our crops and our economy would really feel the sting!

Your Turn Reread paragraph 1 on page 73.

- What is the key idea of the paragraph? ______________________

____

____

- How does the key idea and what you know about bees help you determine the meaning of the pun? ______________________

____

____

Readers to Writers

If you want to use puns in your writing, you can find ideas for puns in books or online, or you can write your own. However, choose carefully. Make sure a pun says what you intend it to say and that your readers will understand the play on words.

Try writing a pun.

____

____

____

____

____

____

Integrate **MAKE CONNECTIONS**

Text Connections

How does the speaker in the poem and the authors of *The Case of the Missing Bees* and "Busy, Beneficial Bees" help you understand their point of view about how humans and animals affect each other?

Talk About It Read the poem. Talk with a partner about who the speaker is talking to and what the message is.

Cite Text Evidence **Circle** words and phrases in the poem that tell what the speaker asks children not to do. **Underline** how the speaker says the animals will react to kindness. Think about this point of view and how it compares to the points of view of the authors of the selections you read this week.

Write I know how the speaker and the authors feel about how humans and animals interact because ________

____

____

____

____

____

____

____

Quick Tip

As you read the poem, picture the setting and each animal performing its action. This will help you to feel and understand the speaker's point of view.

Kindness to Animals

Little children, never give
Pain to things that feel and live:
Let the gentle robin come
For the crumbs you save at home,—
As his meat you throw along
He'll repay you with a song;
Never hurt the timid hare
Peeping from her green grass lair,
Let her come and sport and play
On the lawn at close of day.

— Anonymous

Accuracy and Rate

Reading aloud text with accuracy means reading each word or number as it appears and pronouncing words correctly. You may need to adjust your rate to read more slowly so that the words are clear and correct.

Quick Tip

Before you read aloud, look at the text. See what kind of text it is so you can plan your rate. You might want to read scientific information more slowly to give yourself time to accurately read difficult words.

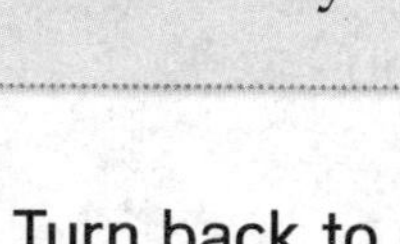
Page 59

In Florida, for example, about 2,000 species of familiar plants and animals are nonnative. These include oranges, chickens, and sugarcane. In fact, 90 percent of farm sales can be traced directly to nonnative species.

Think about where the word breaks and how to say each syllable.

Think about how to read the word for a number.

Your Turn Turn back to page 60. Take turns reading the second paragraph of "A Growing Problem" with a partner. Think about how to read words with multiple syllables and scientific terms. Plan your rate of reading so that you can read with accuracy.

Afterward, think about how you did. Complete these sentences.

I remembered to ______________________________

____

____

Next time, I will ______________________________

____

____

WRITING

TIME

The Case of the MISSING BEES

Essential Question

How do natural events and human activities affect the environment?

Read two views about how natural events and human activities have affected honeybee colonies.

Are Pesticides to Blame?

A study of hives hit by CCD in Florida and California found 50 different human-made chemicals in the samples. The study could not confirm that the pesticides had directly caused CCD, but other scientists are still investigating whether pesticides are at least partly to blame. At the least, the chemicals may weaken bees enough to allow infection by a virus or a fungus. Until scientists know the exact cause of the honeybee disappearance, the use of these harsh poisons should be cut back.

Respond to the Text

1. Use details from the selection to summarize.
2. Think about how each argumentative article is organized. Which author's style is more convincing and why?
3. What do you think caused the bees to disappear? Support your answer with reasons. How could people help honeybees?

Literature Anthology: pages 386–389

Expert Model

Features of an Opinion Essay

An opinion essay is a form of an argumentative text. Opinion essays try to persuade readers to agree with the author's opinion. An opinion essay

- introduces a clearly stated opinion
- includes reasons, facts, details, and evidence that support the author's opinion
- includes a strong conclusion to convince the intended audience to agree with the author's opinion

Analyze an Expert Model Studying argumentative texts will help you learn how to plan and write an opinion. **Reread** "A Germ of an Idea" on **Literature Anthology** page 387. Write your answers to the questions below.

What is the author's opinion about the decline of the honeybee population? ______________________________

____

____

What are some facts and details that the author provides to support this opinion? ______________________________

____

____

Plan: Choose Your Topic

Brainstorm With a partner or group, brainstorm a list of endangered species. If you don't know what species are endangered, or need more ideas, you can quickly research the topic online or in books. Record your list here.

____

____

____

____

Quick Tip

To help you choose a topic, think about an endangered plant or animal that you care about. If you care about your topic, it will come across in your writing and your readers will care, too.

Writing Prompt Choose one endangered species from your list. Write an opinion essay about why this species should be protected and how people can protect it. Include information about why it is endangered.

I will write about ______________________________

____

Purpose and Audience Think about who will read or hear your essay. Will your purpose be to inform, persuade, or entertain them? Is there more than one purpose? Then think about how you will support the purpose of your essay.

My audience will be ______________________________

I will use ____________________ to support the purpose of my essay.

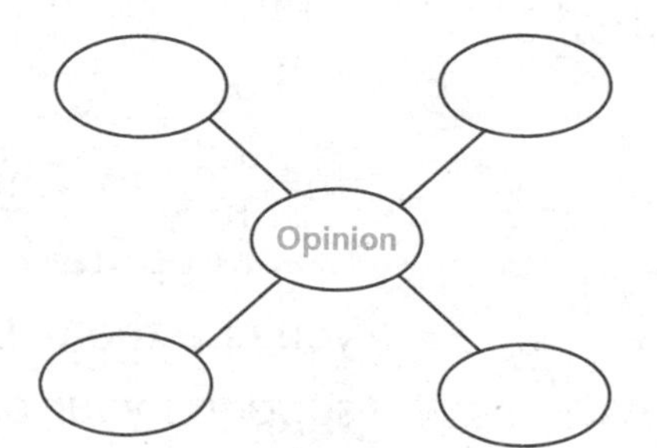

Plan In your writer's notebook, make an Opinion web to plan your writing. Fill in the Opinion oval.

WRITING

Plan: Develop Support

Find Supporting Information Once you form your opinion, you will need to find plenty of facts to support it. To do this, you will need to research your topic. Make sure you choose reliable sources, such as books, periodicals, and trustworthy websites. As you read your sources and take notes, think about these questions:

- Is this information relevant to my topic?
- Are there facts, examples, and details that support my opinion?
- Is my source reliable and up to date?

List two pieces of supporting information for your essay.

1 ____

____

2 ____

____

Take Notes Check that you have correctly copied any quotes you plan to use. Keep track of your sources in case you need to refer to them when you cite them. Look over your notes, choose the information that best supports your opinion, and use it to fill in your Opinon Web.

Digital Tools

For more information about how to take notes, watch the "Take Notes: Print" tutorial. Go to **my.mheducation.com**.

Draft

Strong Conclusion In an opinion essay, it is especially important to have a strong conclusion. The goal is to leave the reader thinking about the topic and agreeing with the opinion. In the example below from "What Is the Future of the Rain Forests?" the author concludes with a strong statement clearly stating an opinion about the rain forests and what must be done to save them.

> Nations must look beyond local needs. They must adopt a global perspective. We need to preserve the rain forests for the benefit of all.

Word Wise

Notice that the conclusion from "What Is the Future of the Rain Forests?" includes strong words such as "must" and "need." These kinds of words clearly communicate the author's opinion.

Now use the paragraph above as a model to draft a conclusion you might use.

____

____

____

____

____

____

____

Write a Draft Use your Opinion graphic organizer to help you write your draft in your writer's notebook. Make sure to include the characteristics of an opinion essay such as having a clearly stated opinion and details that support that opinion. As you finish your draft, think about if you need to add or change anything to the conclusion you wrote above.

Revise

Sentence Structure Effective writers make sure that their sentence structure clearly communicates their ideas. Sometimes combining ideas can make your sentences clearer. You can also improve the sentence structure by rearranging, or moving, ideas in the sentence.

Here is an example: *Sally knows the dog is big, she knows the dog is brown, and the dog lives next door.* These phrases all describe things Sally knows about the same dog, so they can be combined. *Sally knows the dog next door is big and brown.* This makes it clear that the writer is talking about the same dog that lives next door.

Read the sentence below. How might you revise it to combine ideas? Do you need to change the order of any ideas?

Pythons are a threat to native species in Florida, and these species are endangered.

____

____

Revision Revise your draft. Check that your sentences are clear. Combine and rearrange ideas for clarity as needed. This will also make your writing more enjoyable to read.

Quick Tip

Read your sentences aloud. Do they make sense? Are the ideas clear and easy to follow? If not, you may need to rearrange or combine ideas.

Christopher Futcher/Getty Images

Peer Conferences

Review a Draft Listen carefully as a partner reads his or her work aloud. Take notes about what you liked and what was difficult to follow. Begin by telling what you liked about the draft. Ask questions that will help the writer think more about the writing. Make suggestions that you think will make the writing stronger. Use these sentence starters.

I enjoyed this part of your draft because. . .

You could add more support for the idea that. . .

I have a question about. . .

I thought the conclusion was. . .

Partner Feedback After your partner gives you feedback on your draft, write one of the suggestions that you will use in your revision. Refer to the rubric on page 85 as you give feedback.

Based on my partner's feedback, I will ______________________________

____

____

____

After you finish giving each other feedback, reflect on the peer conference. What was helpful? What might you do differently next time?

Revision As you revise your draft, use the Revising Checklist to help you figure out what text you may need to move, elaborate on, or delete. Remember to use the rubric on page 85 to help you with your revision.

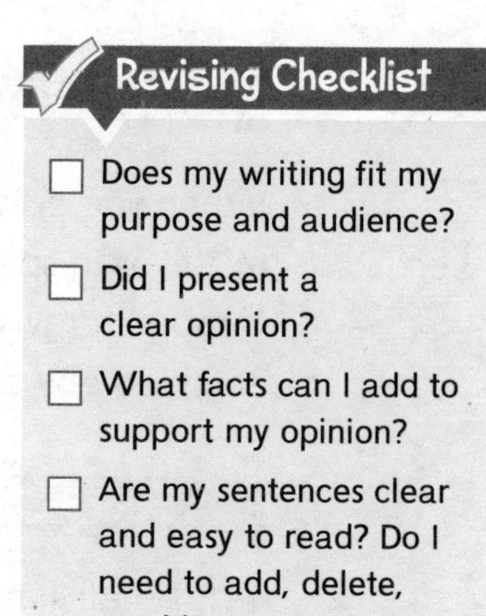

Edit and Proofread

When you **edit** and **proofread** your writing, you look for and correct mistakes in spelling, punctuation, capitalization, and grammar. Reading through a revised draft multiple times can help you make sure you're catching any errors. Use the checklist below to edit your sentences.

Grammar Connection

When you proofread your opinion essay, make sure that there is agreement between subjects and verbs. For instance: *The animal swims. The animals swim.*

Editing Checklist

- ☐ Do all sentences begin with a capital letter and end with a punctuation mark?
- ☐ Are there any run-on sentences or sentence fragments?
- ☐ Are past tenses of irregular verbs used correctly?
- ☐ Are proper nouns capitalized?
- ☐ Are the comparative and superlative forms of adjectives used correctly?
- ☐ Are all words spelled correctly?

List two mistakes you found as you proofread your opinion essay.

1. ____

____

2. ____

____

Publish, Present, and Evaluate

Publishing When you **publish** your writing, you create a clean, neat final copy that is free of mistakes. Adding visuals can make your writing more interesting. Consider including illustrations, photos, or maps to help make your opinion essay more interesting.

Presentation When you are ready to **present** your work, rehearse your presentation. Use the Presenting Checklist to help you.

Evaluate After you publish your writing, use the rubric below to **evaluate** your writing.

What did you do successfully? ______________________________

What needs more work? ______________________________

____

Presenting Checklist

- ☐ Make eye contact with the audience. This will help your audience stay engaged with what you are saying.
- ☐ Speak clearly, slowly, and loud enough to be heard.
- ☐ Display any visuals so that everyone can see them.
- ☐ Answer questions thoughtfully, using details from your topic.

4	3	2	1
• clearly states an opinion about the topic in an interesting and engaging way • includes plenty of supporting information such as reasons, facts, details, and evidence • the conclusion is strong and clearly relates to the opinion	• states an opinion on the topic • includes some supporting information such as reasons, facts, details, and evidence • the conclusion relates to the opinion	• the opinion on the topic isn't quite clear • includes few reasons, facts, details, and evidence • the conclusion does not clearly relate to the opinion	• the opinion and topic are not clear • there are no supporting reasons, facts, details, or evidence • there is no conclusion

SHOW WHAT YOU LEARNED

Spiral Review

You have learned new skills and strategies in Unit 5 that will help you read more critically. Now it is time to practice what you have learned.

- Cause and Effect
- Author's Point of View
- Root Words
- Make Inferences
- Compare and Contrast
- Imagery
- Idioms

Connect to Content

- Foreshadowing
- Research About the New Deal
- Is Anybody Out There?

Read two different views about a topic and choose the best answer to each question.

Wolves in YELLOWSTONE

1 During the 1800s, packs of wolves roamed through Yellowstone National Park. However, by the end of the 1920s, most of the wolves had been killed by hunters. Scientists spent years wondering about the effects of the lost population of wolves on Yellowstone's ecosystem.

2 In 1995, scientists decided to add wolves back into the Yellowstone environment. Some thought the wolves would bring good changes to the large population of elk–a kind of deer–and low population of beavers in the park. But not everyone agreed. Some worried that the population of elk might suffer and nearby livestock might be in danger.

Argument 1: Wolves are good for Yellowstone.

3 Wolves help prevent certain animal groups from overpopulating. In a food chain, the population of animals is affected by the diets and behaviors of other animals. When one animal, such as the wolf, disappears, many other animals in the chain can be affected. When the wolves were gone, an important predator for elk was also lost.

Wolves are predators who feed on elk. As a result, the population of elk became too large. They did not move around as much because they were no longer afraid of wolves. When a large number of elk stayed in one place too long, they ate too many willow plants. Beavers also need willow plants to eat and to build dams. With few willow plants left to help beavers stay alive during winter, the population of beavers began to shrink.

4 After wolves were reintroduced into the park, they helped keep the population of elk at a healthy level. The wolves also helped keep the elk on the move so they did not completely ruin the willow plants. With a high number of willow plants, the population of beavers grew again. Ed Bangs, a wildlife expert, believes that "Wolves mean food" for everyone.

Argument 2: Wolves lead to problems.

5 Not everyone is happy about the wolves being back in Yellowstone. Many hunters are upset. Wolves have killed more than twice as many elk than scientists guessed they would. Some people are afraid that the wolves will eventually kill all the elk, leaving none for the hunters. Ranchers near Yellowstone worry that the wolves will kill their livestock. People are concerned that the wolves would hurt their chances of having food and of making money. Some hunters and ranchers have asked the courts for help to stop the wolf project in Yellowstone. Their problems with wolves are chronic.

6 To address these concerns, some have suggested getting rid of the endangered species label for wolves. This label means that an animal is in danger of becoming extinct or dying out and needs government help to stay alive. Other solutions include giving states control over the number of wolves and to allow for wolf hunting seasons during certain times of the year.

7 There is no easy solution. When figuring out what to do, people must work to balance the best interests of the animals, the environment, and the humans who live there.

Barrett Hedges/National Geographic/Getty Images

SHOW WHAT YOU LEARNED

1. Bringing wolves to Yellowstone is good for the ecosystem because –

   A it would provide another source of food for elk

   B it would control the populations of elk

   C it would let the elk stay in one place

   D it would offer a way to shrink the numbers of willow plants

2. Based on the information in the selection, you can infer that "'Wolves mean food' for everyone" in paragraph 4 means that –

   F hunters should be able to hunt wolves

   G wolves should be able to feed on livestock

   H elks have more food available

   J beavers have more food available

3. The Greek root *chron-* means "time." In paragraph 5, what does chronic mean?

   A continuing for a long time

   B ending soon

   C quickly approaching

   D starting and stopping over a certain period of time

4. Why is paragraph 5 important to the author's claim that wolves lead to problems?

   F It explains why wolves are important to the ecosystem.

   G It tells what the problems are.

   H It gives specific solutions to the problems.

   J It helps readers understand what "endangered" means..

Quick Tip

For multiple-choice questions, rule out the answers that are definitely wrong. Then spend some time focusing on the remaining answers.

Read the selection and choose the best answer to each question.

IN A DUSTY KITCHEN

1 Maria coughed, her lungs burning, as she swept the dust from the floor of the family kitchen. She carefully poured each scoop of dust into a waiting basket. To keep the dust in the air from getting into her lungs and eyes, she pulled a worn cotton scarf over her face. Briefly, she paused and wondered why she bothered with these tasks. The dust was endless in 1935 in this part of Texas. "I'll help you sweep in a minute," her mother smiled sadly. "This dust is getting out of hand. I can hardly think straight. It's hard for the baby, and I'm worried about grandmother's cough. I'm going to go check on her."

2 The region where Maria and her family lived was part of the Dust Bowl, an area where the lack of rain combined with wind and dust storms had made it nearly impossible to grow crops or keep livestock. This situation produced a weather condition called a drought. Cattle had overeaten the natural grasses in the area, leaving the dry land helpless to the power of the wind. Many cattle did not survive because they couldn't breathe the dusty air. The cattle rancher that Maria's family worked for had lost both his money and his farm.

3 Many of Maria's neighbors spoke of packing their belongings and moving to California in search of work on farms. No one wanted to leave Texas, but the dust made it extremely difficult to live there. Maria had heard just yesterday that her best friend Diego and his family were leaving soon.

Photo by George E. Marsh, NOAA, Dept. of Commerce

SHOW WHAT YOU LEARNED

4 Thinking about Diego's parting made Maria sad. She wanted to do something to say goodbye and to help all the families remember the lives they had led here together. But a party seemed out of the question. Each family had so little food right now. She continued her battle with the broom against the dust, but a rumble in her stomach reminded Maria of her grandmother's delicious tamales—meat or other fillings wrapped in a dough made of cornmeal and then steamed in corn husks.

5 Then Maria noticed the tin of cornmeal sitting on the kitchen shelf above her head. She thought, we don't have all the ingredients for tamales, but we have some of them. Maybe other families have some of the ingredients, too. We could have a *tamalada*—a tamale-making party. We could ask Diego's family, the rancher's family, and others to bring what they have. What better way than a community feast to send everyone on their journeys with good wishes for a plentiful future? Maria set the broom aside and reached for the tin of cornmeal. Then she went to find her mother. There was an important going-away party to plan.

1 Which of the following sentences uses imagery to show how bad the dust is?

A Maria coughed, her lungs burning, as she swept the dust from the floor of the family kitchen.

B This situation produced a weather condition called a drought.

C No one wanted to leave Texas, but the dust made it extremely difficult to live here.

D There was an important going-away party to plan.

2 In paragraph 2, the author contrasts the setting before and after the drought sets in to show the effects of —

F planting too much grassland

G breathing in too much dust

H keeping too much livestock

J cattle overeating grass

3 What can you infer about both Maria and her mother?

A They both care about others.

B They are both very sad that Diego's family is leaving.

C They both want to move to California to escape the dust storm.

D They both know how to make tamales.

4 What is the meaning of the idiom getting out of hand in paragraph 1?

F falling on the floor

G blowing in the wind

H becoming a big problem

J gathering in piles

Quick Tip

For multiple-choice questions, try to answer the question before reading the answer options. Then match your answer to the best option.

EXTEND YOUR LEARNING

COMPARING GENRES

COLLABORATE

- In the **Literature Anthology,** reread the expository text *When Is a Planet Not a Planet?* on pages 346-361 and the argumentative text *The Case of the Missing Bees* on pages 386-389.
- Use the Venn Diagram to show how the two genres are the same and different. Include information about the author's purpose and text structure.

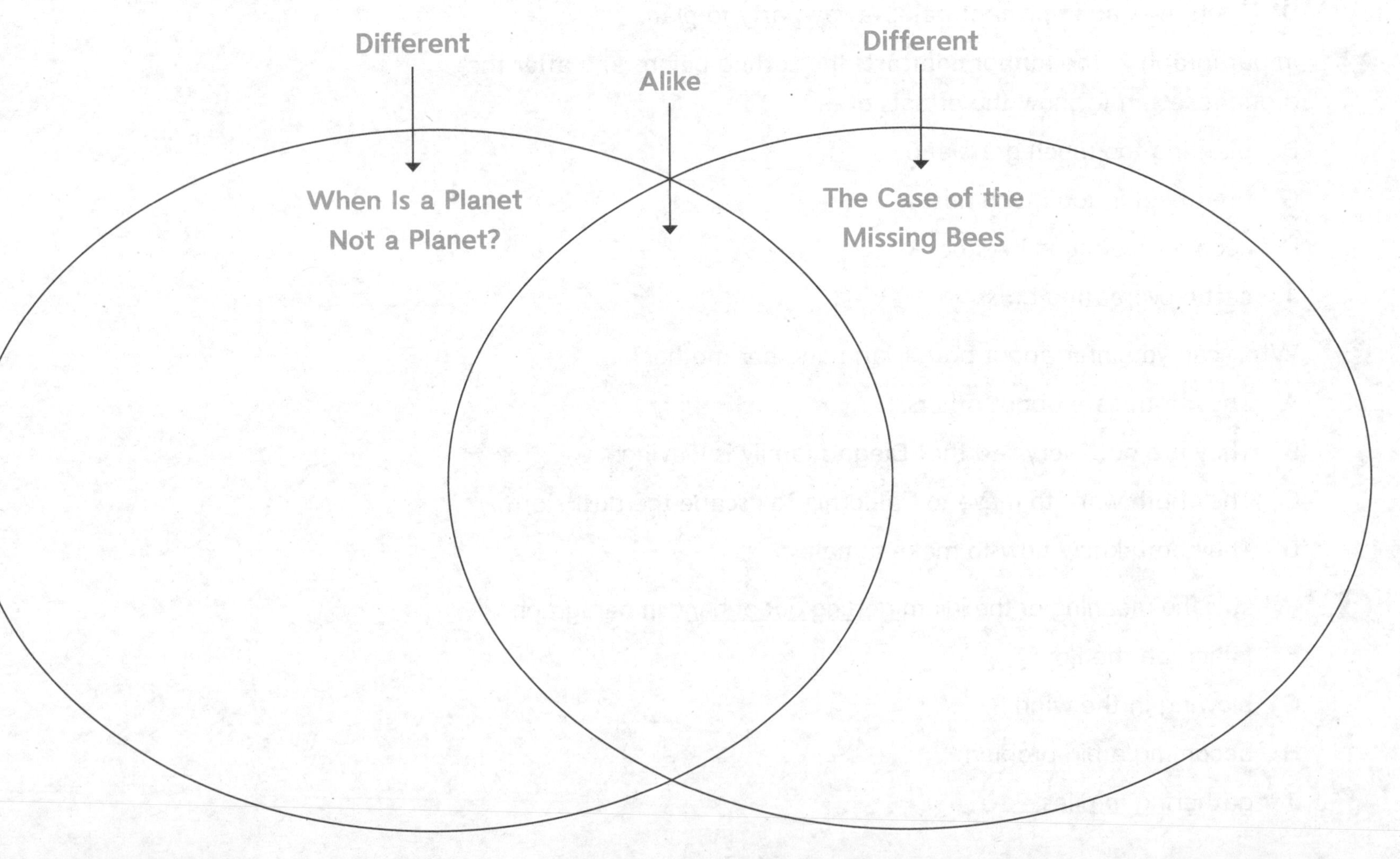

HISTORICAL SETTING

The setting of a story is the time and place of action. A historical setting, such as the Great Depression (1929–1939), comes from a real time period in history. An author may reveal a historical setting through details such as clothing, entertainment, dialect, idioms, and other cultural practices.

- Reread *Bud, Not Buddy,* pages 366–369 of the **Literature Anthology**. Pay close attention to the setting and the plot.
- Then read one or more historical accounts about the Great Depression and make notes in your notebook about information that relates to *Bud, Not Buddy*.
- Use your notes to help you analyze the influence of the setting on the plot. Record your ideas on the chart below.

Historical Setting: The Great Depression	Influence on the Plot

EXTEND YOUR LEARNING

FORESHADOWING

Foreshadowing occurs when an author gives hints or clues about future plot events. Foreshadowing is a literary device that helps the reader make predictions or develop expectations about the way the plot will unfold.

By the end of the excerpt of *Bud, Not Buddy,* Bud has found a new home. What details at the beginning of the historical fiction piece, including page 367 in the **Literature Anthology**, foreshadow this resolution?

____

____

____

RESEARCH ABOUT THE NEW DEAL

During the Great Depression, President Franklin D. Roosevelt tried to help people survive with a series of programs known as the New Deal. Some of these programs were the Civilian Conservation Corps (CCC), the Works Progress Administration (WPA), the Public Works Administration (PWA), and the Social Security Act.

- Research one New Deal program. Use focused research questions. What was the program? When did it start and end? How did it help people?
- Choose a genre for presenting your research. When choosing your genre, think about who your audience is. Plan your first draft by mapping your ideas in an idea web. Edit your work and present it to an audience.

Something I learned while working on this presentation is ______________

____

IS ANYBODY OUT THERE?

Log on to **my.mheducation.com** and reread the *Time for Kids* online article "Is Anybody Out There?" including the information found in the interactive elements. Evaluate the details to help you determine key ideas. This will help you answer the questions below.

Is Anybody Out There?

Is there a planet similar to Earth orbiting a star in distant galaxy? Most likely, say astronomers.

It took humans thousands of years to discover the planets circling our own little sun. Here's a big question: Were there similar planets orbiting their own suns among the hundreds of billions of stars in our galaxy? No one knew the answer to that mystery until 1995. That's when astronomers found the first planet to orbit a distant star other than our sun. Such a planet is called

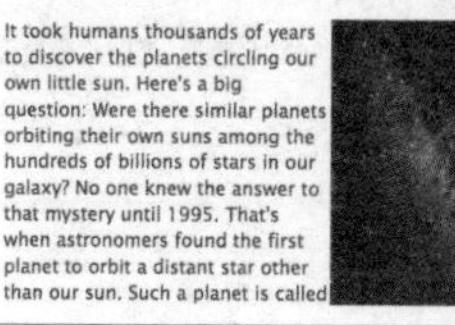

Time for Kids: "Is Anybody Out There?"

- What affects whether life is possible on a planet in a star's "Goldilocks region"?

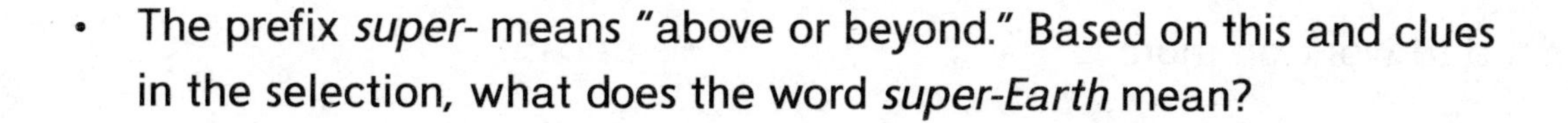

- The prefix *super-* means "above or beyond." Based on this and clues in the selection, what does the word *super-Earth* mean?

- What have scientists discovered on Earth that has caused the Goldilocks zone to grow wider?

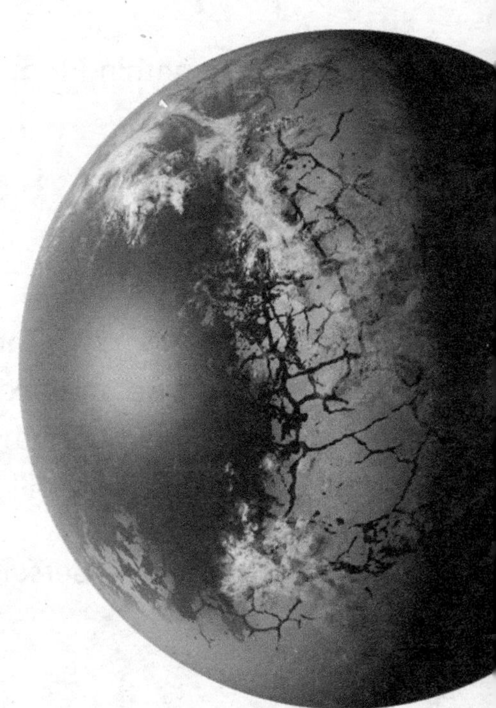

NASA/JPL-Caltech

TRACK YOUR PROGRESS

WHAT DID YOU LEARN?

Use the rubric to evaluate yourself on the skills you learned in this unit. Write your scores below.

4	3	2	1
I can successfully identify all examples of this skill.	I can identify most examples of this skill.	I can identify a few examples of this skill.	I need to work on this skill more.

☐ Cause and Effect
☐ Compare and Contrast
☐ Greek Roots
☐ Author's Point of View
☐ Idioms
☐ Root Words

Something that I need to work on more is ________________ because

____

____

____

Text to Self Think back over the texts that you have read in this unit. Choose one text and write a short paragraph explaining a personal connection that you have made to the text. Making a personal connection will help to deepen your understanding of the text.

I made a personal connection to ______________ because ______________

____

____

____

Integrate **RESEARCH AND INQUIRY**

SCIENCE

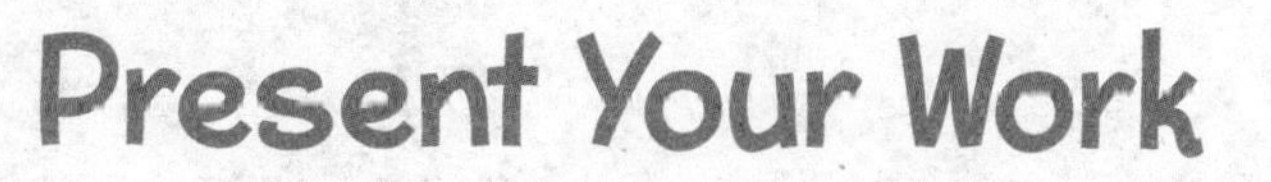

Present Your Work

Discuss how you will present your mock Blog Report on an invasive species, including how you will present any photos, videos, or sounds that are part of your report. Discuss the sentence starters below and write your answers.

Use the Listening Checklist as your classmates give their presentation.

After learning more about invasive species in the United States, I discovered ______________________________

____

____

I would like to know more about ______________________________

____

____

Tech Tip

If you include hyperlinks in your blog, check that they work correctly before your presentation.

Listening Checklist

- ☐ Listen actively by taking notes on the presenter's ideas.
- ☐ Pay attention to nonverbal cues such as pointing and other gestures. This will help you to better understand the information being presented.
- ☐ Ask relevant questions.
- ☐ Provide feedback and make pertinent comments.

Klaus Vedfelt/Digital Vision/Getty Images

Talk About It

Essential Question

How do different groups contribute to a cause?

When the United States joined the fight in World War II, people all over the country were called on to make contributions to the war effort. Many factories stopped making their usual products and started to make equipment that was needed more, such as airplanes.

Look at the photo. What are the women doing? Talk with a partner about words and phrases that have to do with contributing to a cause. Write your ideas in the web.

SOCIAL STUDIES

Contributing to a Cause

Go online to **my.mheducation.com** and read the "Outstanding Contributions" Blast. Think about what makes a contribution outstanding and why. Why is it sometimes important to make a contribution? Then blast back your response.

TAKE NOTES

To help you focus as you read, preview the text and pay attention to genre characteristics. Make a prediction about the narrator, Libby Kendall. Read the title and the Essential Question. Preview the illustrations, and read the first paragraph. Write your prediction here.

____

____

____

As you read, make note of:

Interesting Words ______________________________

____

____

____

Key Details ______________________________

____

____

____

____

SHIPPED OUT

Essential Question

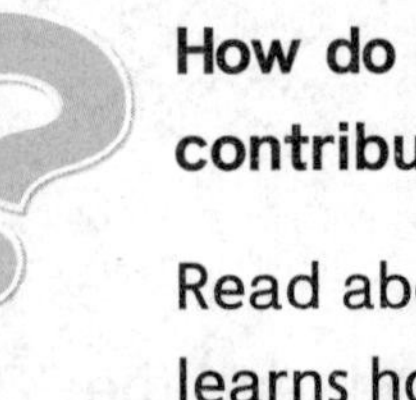

How do different groups contribute to a cause?

Read about how a young girl learns how to contribute to the war effort during World War II.

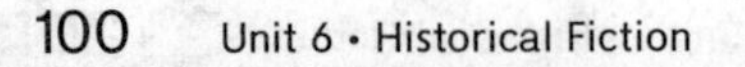

My name is Libby Kendall, and I am a prisoner of war. Well, not really, but some days it feels that way. Just like my dad, I've packed up my things and shipped out. Unlike my dad, however, nothing I do will ever help the Allies win World War II.

My father is a mechanic on a battleship in the Pacific Ocean. I'm trapped in a little apartment above my Aunt Lucia's bakery downtown. Mom says it's just for a few months while she works double shifts at the clothing factory. She makes uniforms, mostly sewing pockets on jackets. I asked her once if she snuck things into the pockets for soldiers to find, like little poems written in calligraphy. She said soldiers wore jackets with pockets to hold tools they might need for war **survival,** not silly things like poetry.

It seems no one appreciates my creative **contributions** to the war effort, but Aunt Lucia says my help to her is important, since both her workers joined the army.

On my first day with Aunt Lucia, she explained the daily **operations** of the bakery. First, we get up before dawn to knead the dough. Next, we bake breads and muffins. Then, while I help customers, Lucia makes cakes and cookies for sale in the afternoon. Whenever the phone rings, she races from the back room to **intercept** the call. She's always worried that it might be bad news, so she wants to be the first to hear it.

After dinner, Aunt Lucia invites neighbors over to listen to the radio. Some are immigrants from a wide **diversity** of backgrounds. Lucia and others help translate the news into several languages for everyone to understand. I always listen closely for any **bulletin** about fighting in the Pacific.

HISTORICAL FICTION

FIND TEXT EVIDENCE

Read

Paragraphs 1–2

Theme

What information supports the idea that different people can contribute to a cause? **Underline** the text evidence. Write your answer here.

Paragraphs 3–5

Summarize

Circle the key details that describe Libby's work. Summarize it here.

Reread

Author's Craft

This story uses a first-person point of view. How does that affect the mood of the story?

SHARED READ

FIND TEXT EVIDENCE

Read

Paragraphs 1–3

Flashback

Circle clues that show Libby is thinking about an earlier time.

Paragraph 3

Theme

Underline text evidence that shows the change in Libby's behavior after she learns her dad is joining the navy.

Paragraph 4

Summarize

Summarize how Libby responds to her feelings.

____

____

____

Reread

Author's Craft

Why did the author include the flashback in this story?

I remember how intently my parents read reports about the war, which I rarely understood. They often whispered to one another, and I'd shout out something like, "Speak up! I can't hear you!" They'd frown and leave me alone to talk in private.

One night, they came into the living room and turned off the radio. At first I was angry, but they had serious expressions on their faces. "Our country's at war," Dad said. "The military will be looking for new **recruits**. I know something about boats and ship engines, so I intend to join the navy."

My face grew hot, but my hands felt cold. "You can't just leave," I said. I stomped on the floor for emphasis and stormed off to my bedroom. Looking back on that now, I feel ashamed of how selfishly I had acted.

This morning, Aunt Lucia can tell I'm feeling down. She asks me to help her decorate cupcakes for a fundraiser tonight. At first I'm not interested. I just slather on frosting and plop a berry on top. Then I realize that I can make red stripes out of strawberries and a patch of blue from blueberries. Soon I have a whole tray of cupcakes decorated like flags to show Aunt Lucia.

"These are wonderful!" Lucia says. "I'm sure they'll sell better than anything else!"

For the first time in weeks, I feel like I've done something right. I think of all the money we might make at the sale, and how it may buy supplies for my father.

"I **enlisted** in the navy to help restore democracy in the world," my dad said on the day he left. "Now you be a good navy daughter and sail straight, young lady."

I promised I would. As he went out the door, I slipped a little poem into his coat pocket. "Here's a little rhyme to pass the day," it said. "I love you back in the U.S.A.!"

I look at the cupcakes and wish I could send one to my dad. Instead, I'll draw a platter on which they're piled high and send the picture off to the Pacific with a letter. That way, my dad will have plenty to share with everyone there.

Summarize

Use your notes to summarize the events in the story. Be sure to include details about the plot elements. Tell whether your prediction on page 100 was confirmed.

HISTORICAL FICTION

FIND TEXT EVIDENCE

Read

Paragraphs 1–2

Theme

How does Aunt Lucia try to cheer up Libby? What effect does this have?

Paragraphs 2–5

Homophones

Underline context clues that help you distinguish the meanings of *sale* and *sail*. Write their meanings.

Reread

Author's Craft

What message does the author give readers through Libby's actions?

Vocabulary

Use the example sentences to talk with a partner about each word. Then answer the questions.

bulletin

Kip posted a **bulletin** in the neighborhood about his missing dog.

Why else might you post a bulletin?

____

____

contributions

The art exhibit at school will feature **contributions** by many student artists.

What other events depend on contributions from others?

____

____

diversity

There was a great **diversity** of breeds at the dog show.

Where else might you see a large diversity of animals?

____

____

enlisted

Citizens who have **enlisted** in the military are sworn in before training begins.

Why might people enlist in the military?

____

____

intercept

I jumped up to **intercept** the pass and to prevent a touchdown by the other team.

In what other sports might you intercept a ball?

____

Build Your Word List Pick a word you found interesting in the selection you read. Look up synonyms and antonyms of the word in a thesaurus and write them in your writer's notebook.

operations

The crew began **operations** to clean up after the disaster.

What other operations might help after a disaster?

______

______

______

recruits

The official addressed the new **recruits**.

What kinds of organizations look for new recruits?

______

______

______

survival

Food and water are important for **survival** during an emergency.

What other items are important for survival during an emergency?

______

______

______

Homophones

Sometimes when you read, you come across **homophones**, or words that sound the same but are spelled differently and have different meanings. Surrounding words and sentences can help you figure out the meaning of a homophone.

FIND TEXT EVIDENCE

In "Shipped Out" on page 101, I see the words war *and* wore, *which are pronounced the same way. From the surrounding words, I can tell that* war *means "a large conflict," and that* wore *is the past tense of the irregular verb* wear, *which means "to have clothing on."*

She said soldiers wore jackets with pockets to hold tools they might need for war survival, not silly things like poetry.

Your Turn Use context clues to distinguish between the meanings of the following homophones from "Shipped Out."

need and **knead,** *page 101* ______

______

read and **red,** *page 102* ______

______

Summarize

Summarizing can help readers evaluate details to determine key ideas as they read. It is important to summarize the story in logical order, starting at the beginning, to help you better understand the setting and plot events. Remember that a summary should not include your opinions.

Quick Tip

A summary does not include everything from the story. It should include only the most important information.

FIND TEXT EVIDENCE

Summarizing the opening paragraphs of "Shipped Out" on page 101 may help you understand the setting and plot elements of the story.

Page 101

My name is Libby Kendall, and I am a prisoner of war. Well, not really, but some days it feels that way. Just like my dad, I've packed up my things and shipped out. Unlike my dad, however, nothing I do will ever help the Allies win World War II.

The first paragraph introduces Libby Kendall, a girl living during World War II. In the paragraphs that follow, readers learn that because her father has gone off to war and her mother must work long hours, Libby has been sent to live with her Aunt Lucia.

Your Turn Summarize what Libby's father plans to do on page 102.

____

____

____

Flashback

The selection "Shipped Out" is historical fiction. Historical fiction features plot events and settings typical of the past period in which the story takes place. It also features realistic characters who speak and act like people from that period. It may include literary devices such as flashbacks.

Quick Tip

Historical fiction is already set in the past. A flashback takes readers even deeper into the past.

FIND TEXT EVIDENCE

I can tell that "Shipped Out" is historical fiction. The first paragraph mentions a real event, World War II. In a flashback, we learn why Libby, the main character, has to live with her aunt.

Page 102

I remember how intently my parents read reports about the war, which I rarely understood. They often whispered to one another, and I'd shout out something like, "Speak up! I can't hear you!" They'd frown and leave me alone to talk in private.

One night, they came into the living room and turned off the radio. At first I was angry, but they had serious expressions on their faces. "Our country's at war," Dad said. "The military will be looking for new **recruits**. I know something about boats and ship engines, so I intend to join the navy."

My face grew hot, but my hands felt cold. "You can't just leave," I said. I stomped on the floor for emphasis and stormed off to my bedroom. Looking back on that now, I feel ashamed of how selfishly I had acted.

This morning, Aunt Lucia can tell I'm feeling down. She asks me to help her decorate cupcakes for a fundraiser tonight. At first I'm not interested. I just slather on frosting and plop a berry on top. Then I realize that I can make red stripes out of strawberries and a patch of blue from blueberries. Soon I have a whole tray of cupcakes decorated like flags to show Aunt Lucia.

Flashback

Flashbacks describe events and actions that occurred before the main action of the story. Signal words and phrases, such as *once* or *I remember*, may show a character remembering past events.

Your Turn Find the flashback on page 103. How does this flashback differ from the one on page 102?

____

____

____

____

Theme

To identify a story's **theme,** or overall message, consider what the characters say and do. Analyze the characters' relationships and conflicts, or problems. In addition to the main theme, some stories may have multiple themes within them. Think about how characters change as a result of what happens to them to help you infer these themes.

Quick Tip

To find a story's theme, you can also think about a lesson a character learns. What the character learns might be a main theme of the story.

FIND TEXT EVIDENCE

On page 101 of "Shipped Out," Libby says that she feels like a prisoner of war at her aunt's apartment. This is because her father has gone to war and her mother has had to leave for work. Libby feels her efforts are not appreciated, but Aunt Lucia needs her help. These plot events will help me identify the theme.

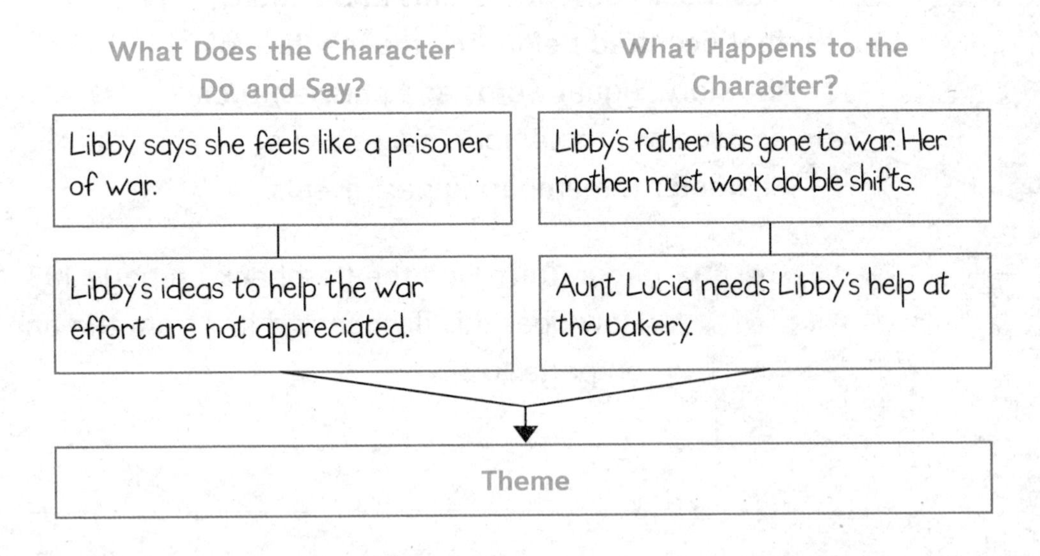

Your Turn What does Libby learn from Aunt Lucia about contributing to the war effort? Add more ideas to the graphic organizer to identify a theme of the story.

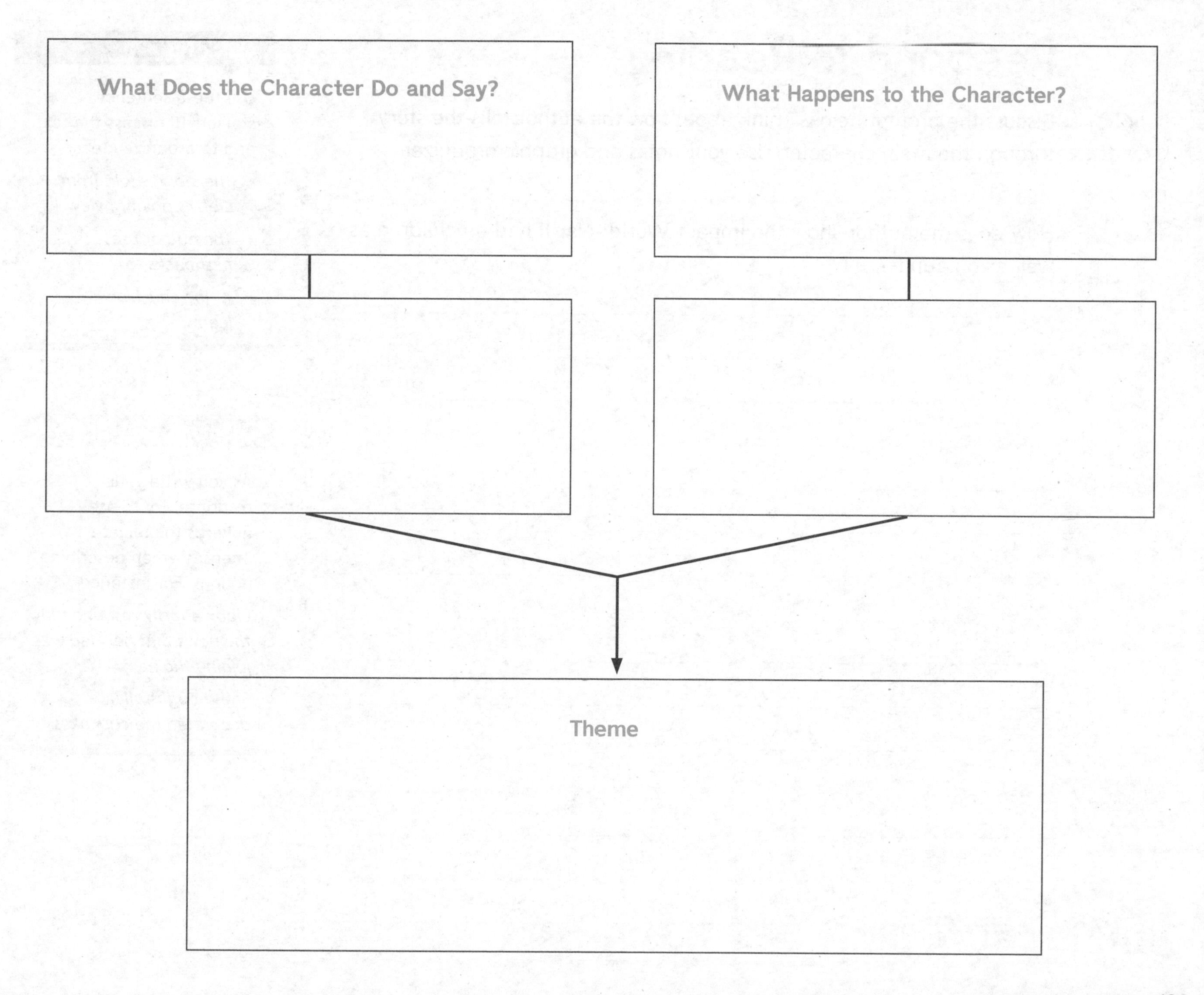
What Does the Character Do and Say?
What Happens to the Character?
Theme

Respond to Reading

Discuss the prompt below. Think about how the author tells the story through the main character. Use your notes and graphic organizer.

How does the author show the impact World War II had on children as well as on adults?

Quick Tip

Use these sentence starters to discuss the text and to organize ideas.

- *The story is told from Libby's point of view. . .*
- *The author uses flashbacks to. . .*
- *At the end, Libby learns. . .*

Grammar Connections

As you write your response, try to use adverbs to indicate intensity when describing actions. For instance:

*Libby **angrily** responded to the news that her dad was joining the navy.*

*She **thoughtfully** decorated the cupcakes.*

Relevant Information

Relevant information contains facts, details, and examples that are about the topic you are researching. Skim, or read quickly, and scan, or search quickly, to find relevant information. You can find information in print or digital texts. Digital texts often have links to other sites or pictures you can click on for more information. As you choose sources, ask yourself:

- Does this information relate closely to my topic?
- Does the information support my purpose for writing?
- Is the information relevant to my audience?

What is another question you might ask about relevant information?

____

____

Create a Cause/Effect Chart With a partner or in a group, research the causes of World War II. If you use digital texts, click on any interactive elements that give more information. Then create a cause/effect chart that shows what you find. Think about these ideas to help focus your research:

- What countries were involved in World War II?
- What happened in these countries before the war started?
- Which countries were invaded, and why were they invaded?

Discuss what information is the most relevant to your topic. Select the strongest details and decide how you want to arrange them on a cause/effect chart.

Quick Tip

If you are having trouble developing a research plan, ask your teacher or school librarian for help. Your teacher or librarian can also help you follow your research plan.

Which of these facts would you include as relevant information for a cause of World War II?

- Germany invades Poland in 1939.
- New York World's Fair opens in 1939.

____

____

____

Reread | ANCHOR TEXT

The Unbreakable Code

Why does Grandfather speak to John in Navajo?

Literature Anthology: pages 430–443

Talk About It Reread **Literature Anthology** pages 432 and 433. Discuss with your partner how the Navajo language is described in the selection.

Cite Text Evidence What words and phrases show the effect the Navajo language has on John? Write text evidence in the web.

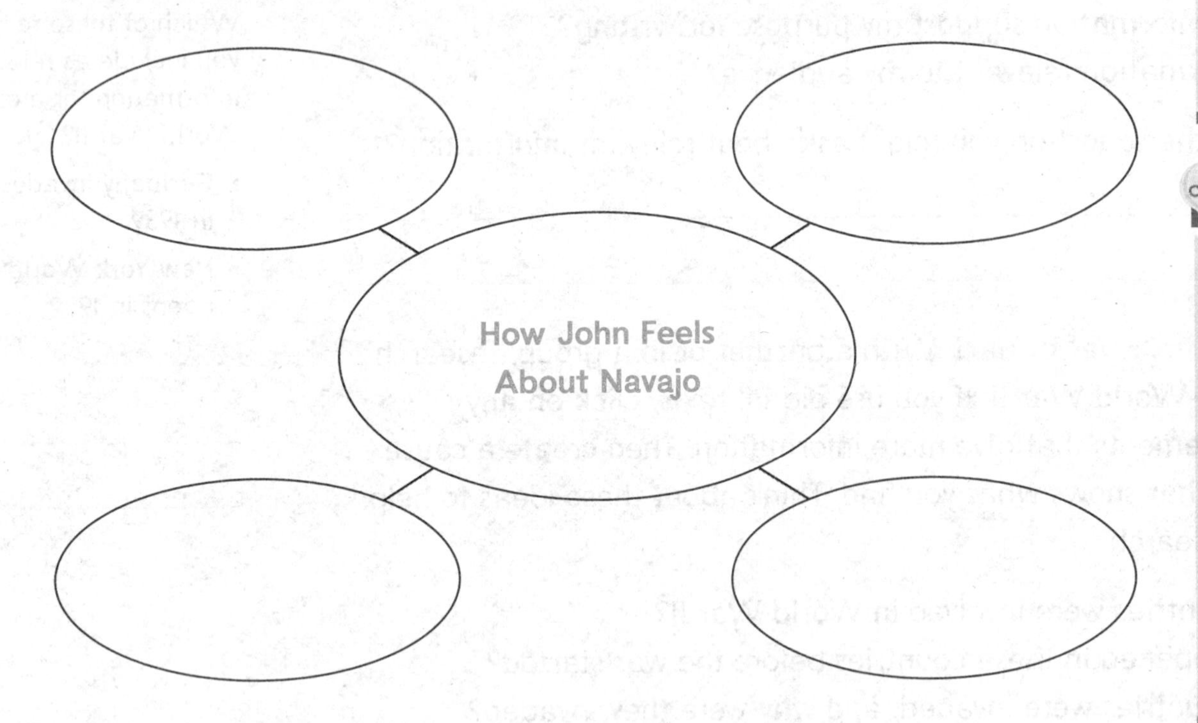

Write Grandfather speaks to John in Navajo because ______________________

____

____

Quick Tip

When you reread, look for words that create mental images, or pictures in your mind. These words can give clues about a character's feelings.

Make Inferences

You can often make inferences based on how characters respond to each other. Think about what they say and what their actions suggest. What inference can you make about how John feels about his school? What does John say and do to help you come to this conclusion?

Why was it important to the story that Grandfather's World War II mission was a secret?

Talk About It Reread **Literature Anthology** pages 436 and 437. Turn to your partner and discuss how the Navajo code is set up.

Cite Text Evidence What words and phrases tell about the secrecy of Grandfather's mission? Write text evidence.

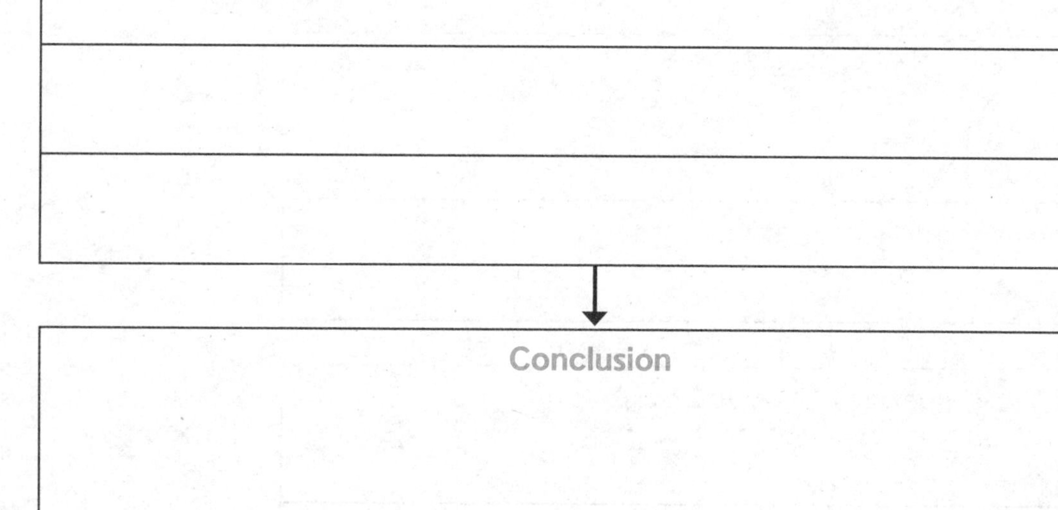

Write It was important to the story that Grandfather's World War II mission was a secret because ______________________

____

____

Quick Tip

The word *secrecy* means "the action of not letting others know something." Thinking about the meaning of this word will help you find text evidence.

Evaluate Information

The author writes that no information could be passed between American ships, planes, and land forces. How does this information help you understand the importance of secrecy during the war?

Reread | ANCHOR TEXT

How does John's reaction to his Grandfather's words show how John has changed?

Talk About It Reread **Literature Anthology** page 443. Turn to a partner and discuss how John has changed by the end of the story.

Cite Text Evidence How does Grandfather's story change the way John feels? Cite evidence from the text in your answer.

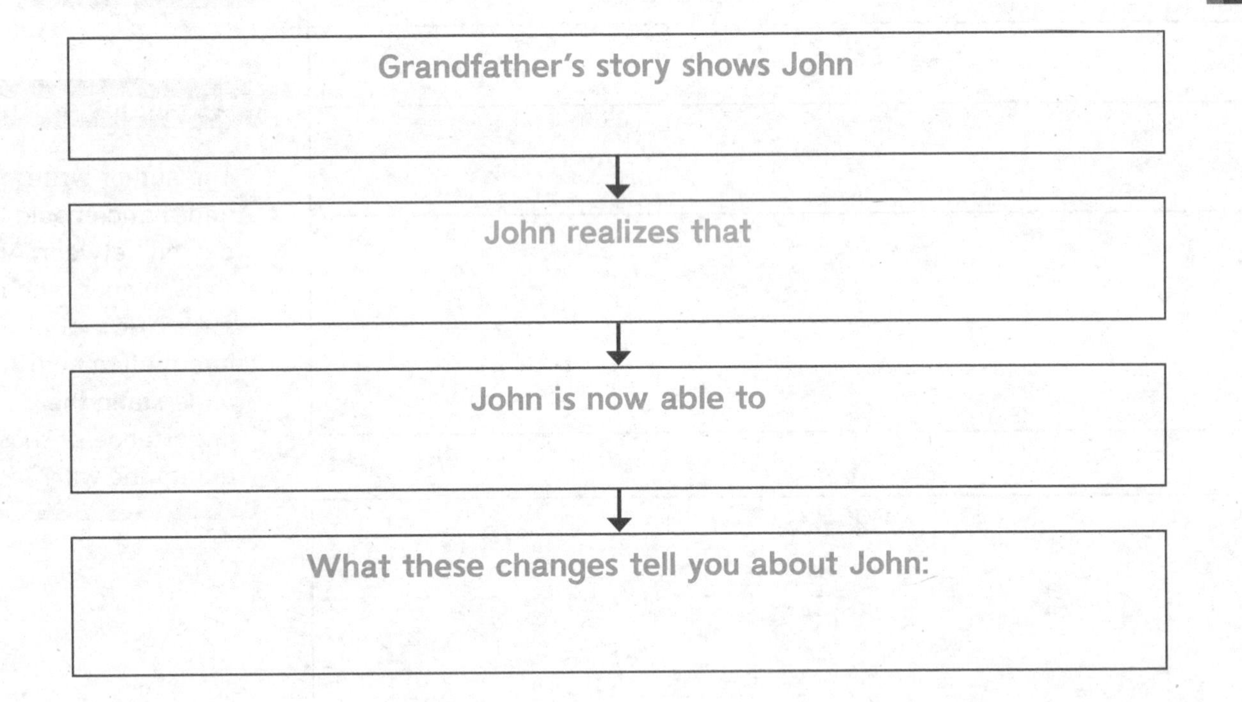

Write By the end of the story, John has changed ______________________

____

____

____

Quick Tip

When you reread, look for words and sentences the author uses to describe the characters' feelings. You can evaluate these details to determine key ideas in the story.

Respond to Reading

Discuss the prompt below. Make connections to your personal experience of different cultures. Use your notes and graphic organizer.

How does the author use dialogue and Grandfather's story to teach John about the strengths of his Navajo culture?

Quick Tip

Use these sentence starters to talk about and cite text evidence.

- *The author includes Grandfather's stories to. . .*
- *John's reaction to these stories shows that. . .*
- *In the end, John. . .*

Self-Selected Reading

Choose a text and write in your writer's notebook the title, author, and genre. Include a personal response to the text in your writer's notebook.

Doug Sherman/Geofile

Reread | PAIRED SELECTION

Allies in Action

Literature Anthology: pages 446–449

Joining the Allies

1 Many men left the United States to fight in the war. Women also enlisted, often serving in the Army Nurse Corps. The large number of recruits that went overseas caused a worker shortage back home. In response, many women took jobs previously held by men. They held positions in government and worked in factories. They also raised funds and collected materials that would be recycled into supplies for the troops.

2 The shortage of workers in agriculture led the United States to institute the Bracero Program with Mexico. Through this program, Mexican laborers worked on farmlands across the United States. These workers helped maintain crops, supporting the country's economy during the war and decades beyond.

Reread paragraph 1. **Underline** a sentence that explains why help from women was needed.

Talk with a partner about why the United States needed the help of women and people from other countries.

Evaluate the details in paragraph 2. **Underline** the details that explain how the Bracero Program worked. Explain why the author included this information in the text.

____

____

____

____

____

____

____

____

The Tuskegee Airmen

3 By the start of the war, a number of African American men were already active in the military. However, their positions were limited. They were rarely given opportunities for advancement and special military operations.

4 Many civil rights groups had protested these restrictions on African Americans. In response, the U.S. Army Air Corps began a new training program in 1941. They taught African Americans how to become pilots and navigators. This program was based in Tuskegee, Alabama. Those who completed aeronautic, or pilot, training there became known as "The Tuskegee Airmen."

5 The Tuskegee Airmen flew many missions during World War II. Over time, they gained a strong reputation for their skills. Their success would lead the U.S. military to recognize African American service and offer them more training opportunities in different fields.

Circle the sentences that tell you that African American soldiers had limited opportunities.

Draw a box around the sentences that explain what happened as a result.

Reread the excerpt on this page. Evaluate the details to determine the key ideas. With a partner, talk about the author's purpose for writing about African Americans in the military during World War II.

Why is it important to know that there were restrictions on African Americans during the war? Use text evidence to support your response.

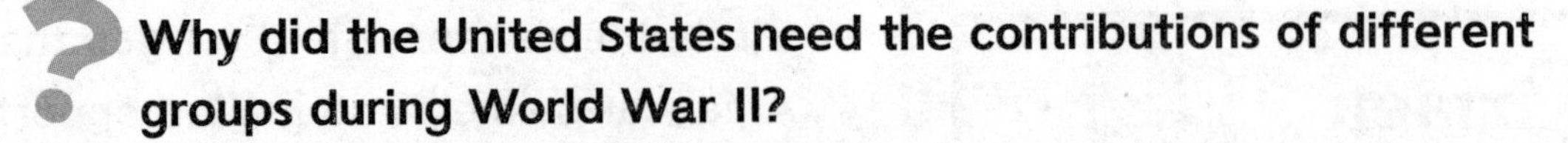

? Why did the United States need the contributions of different groups during World War II?

Talk About It Reread the excerpts on pages 116 and 117. Discuss how the different groups helped the United States and the Allies win the war.

Cite Text Evidence Which groups helped contribute to the war effort? What conclusion can we draw by studying these groups?

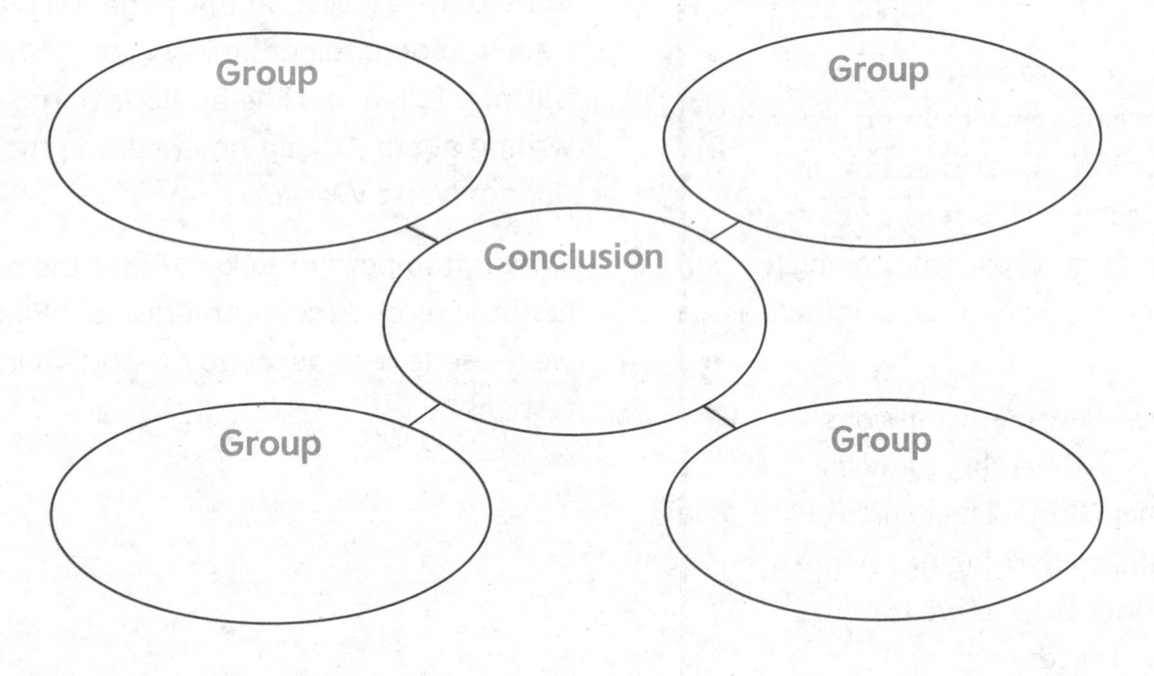

Write The contributions of different groups during the war were needed

because ______________________________

____

____

____

Synthesize Information

In "Allies in Action," the author mentions a number of groups that contributed to the war effort. Consider why the author chose to use these different groups to make a point.

Print and Graphic Features

Authors can choose from many kinds of features to enhance information and help readers better understand the text. Some of these features are headings, maps, charts, photographs, and captions.

FIND TEXT EVIDENCE

On pages 448 and 449 of the **Literature Anthology**, the author of "Allies in Action" uses primary source photographs and captions to illustrate the diverse groups who supported the war effort. The caption below describes the photograph shown on the right.

Nearly 1,000 African Americans completed the pilot training program in Tuskegee, Alabama.

U.S. Air Force photo

Your Turn Analyze the photograph and caption on page 448.

- What was the author's purpose for using a primary source photo in the text?

____

____

- How does the caption add to the text? _______________

____

____

Readers to Writers

Using visual primary sources will make your writing on historical topics come alive. Primary source photos can show the action and the people involved in an event. They can also provide more specific details that are not included in the main text.

Integrate **MAKE CONNECTIONS**

Text Connections

How is the message of this World War II poster similar to the message of *The Unbreakable Code* and "Allies in Action"?

Talk About It Look at the poster and read the caption. Talk with a partner about what the men are doing.

Cite Text Evidence **Underline** clues in the poster that help you understand what the message is. **Circle** evidence in the caption that explains about the poster's purpose.

Write The message of this poster is similar to the message of the selections because ______________________________

____

____

____

____

____

____

____

Quick Tip

Talk about contributions people made to the war effort during World War II. Use details in the poster and ideas you read about to help you.

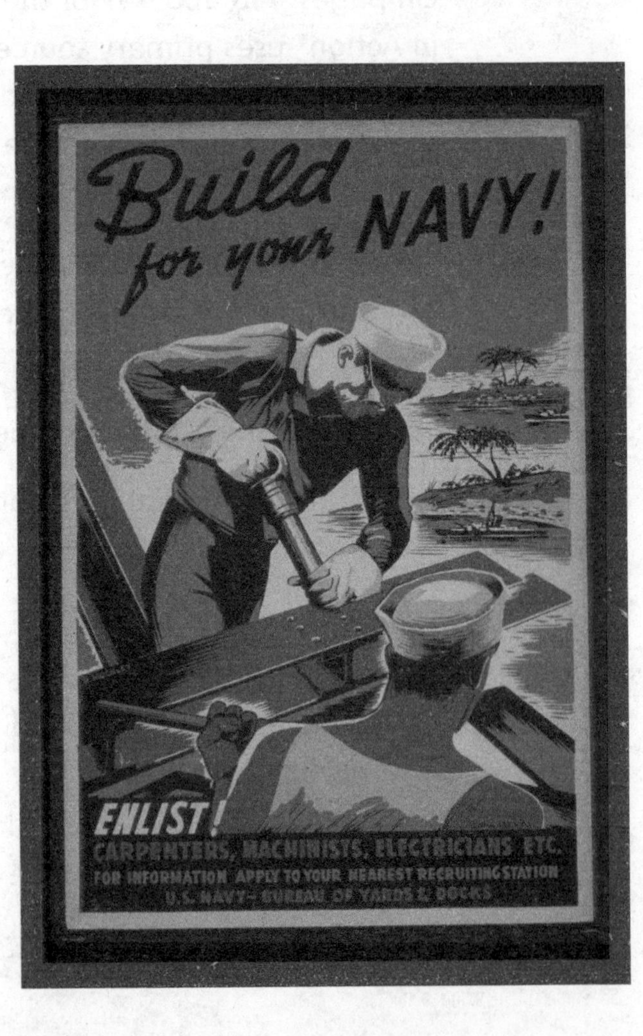

Build for Your Navy! This poster was created by Robert Muchley between 1941 and 1942. It encouraged skilled workers to join the Navy during the war.

Present Your Work

Discuss how you will present your cause/effect chart on the causes of World War II. Use the Presenting Checklist as you practice your presentation. Discuss the sentence starters below and write your answers.

After researching the causes of World War II, I realized ______________________________

I would like to know more about ______________________________

Quick Tip

Plan your rehearsal so that you allow time for questions and feedback. Practice will improve your presentation and give you the confidence to do the best you can.

Presenting Checklist

- ☐ Plan with your partner or group how you will present your chart and each member's role.
- ☐ Speak clearly and with an appropriate rate and volume.
- ☐ Make eye contact.
- ☐ Make sure that everyone in your audience can see your presentation.
- ☐ Allow time for questions. Then provide complete answers.

Literature Anthology: pages 430–443

Expert Model

Features of Historical Fiction

Historical fiction is based on real people, places, or events from the past. However, some details of the story, such as the characters or what the characters say to each other, are made up. Historical fiction

- takes place in the past
- includes some plot events that may have really happened
- tells about events in a logical sequence

Analyze an Expert Model Studying historical fiction will help you learn how to write your own historical fiction story. **Reread** page 439 of *The Unbreakable Code* in the **Literature Anthology**. Write your answers below.

What words and phrases does the author use to help you understand the sequence of events? ______________________________

____

____

What details in the second paragraph tell you that the memory is a difficult one for Grandfather? ______________________________

____

____

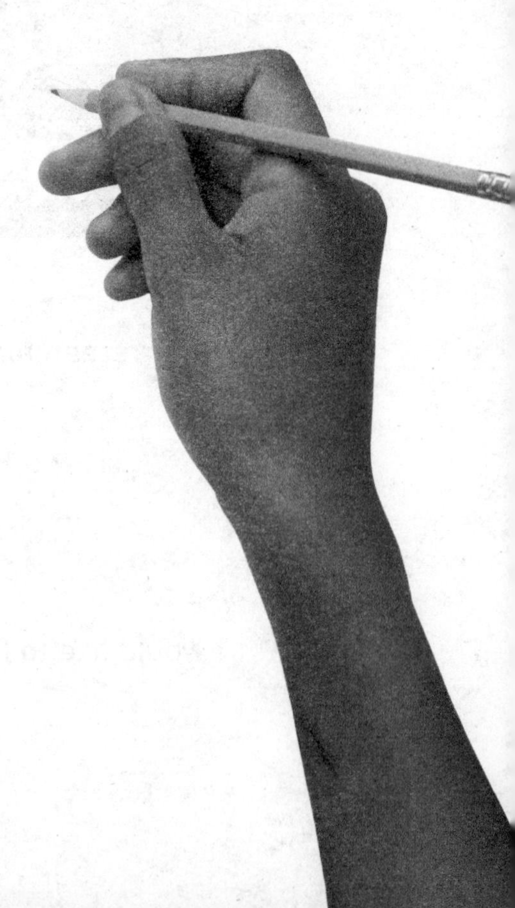

Plan: Choose Your Topic

Mapping With a partner, talk about different periods of history that interest you. Then think about some characters that might live during those times and what they might do. On a sheet of paper, make idea webs of different periods with characters and conflicts they might face.

Writing Prompt Choose one historical period from your idea webs. Write a story about characters from and events that take place during that period in history.

I will write about ______________________________.

Purpose and Audience An **author's purpose** is his or her main reason for writing. What is your purpose for writing? Who will be your audience?

My purpose for writing my story is ______________________________.
____

The audience for my story will be ______________________________.
____

Plan In your writer's notebook, make a Sequence of Events chart to plan your writing. Fill in the first event.

Quick Tip

Authors often use specific words and phrases to help readers understand the sequence of events in a story. Use words or phrases such as *First, Next, After,* and *Finally,* to help readers follow the sequence of events in your story.

First
↓
Next
↓
Then
↓
Last

Plan: Sequence

Sequence of Events When authors write stories, they keep in mind the order of events, or sequence. The sequence in a story helps the reader understand what happens and why it happens. Transition words and phrases signal the sequence of events. Reread the passage from "Shipped Out" and circle the transition words and phrases.

> This morning, Aunt Lucia can tell I'm feeling down. She asks me to help her decorate cupcakes for a fundraiser tonight. At first I'm not interested. I just slather on frosting and plop a berry on top. Then I realize that I can make red stripes out of strawberries and a patch of blue from blueberries. Soon I have a whole tray of cupcakes decorated like flags to show Aunt Lucia.

On the lines below, brainstorm a list of other transition words and phrases. You can reference these as you write your own story to signal the sequence of events.

____

____

____

Take Notes Now go back to your Sequence of Events organizer in your writer's notebook. Fill in the second, third, and fourth event boxes.

Draft

Develop Plot The plot is what happens in a story. It usually includes a conflict, or problem, the characters must solve. Plot elements include rising action, climax, falling action, and resolution. Setting is when and where a story takes place. Think about how the historical setting influences the plot as you read this example from "Shipped Out."

> My name is Libby Kendall, and I am a prisoner of war. Well, not really, but some days it feels that way. Just like my dad, I've packed up my things and shipped out. Unlike my dad, however, nothing I do will ever help the Allies win World War II.

Use the paragraph above for ideas as you begin a paragraph for your story. Introduce specific details about the setting and give clues about the plot.

____

____

____

Write a Draft Use your Sequence of Events graphic organizer to help you write a draft in your writer's notebook. Remember to include a conflict, rising action, a climax, falling action, and a resolution in your draft.

Digital Tools

For information on how to use a story map, watch the "Story Map to Draft" tutorial. Go to **my.mheducation.com.**

Quick Tip

The rising action is when the conflict is introduced. The action during the rising action builds toward the climax, or the high point. This is when the characters face the conflict head on. The falling action happens after the climax. This is when the characters work toward the resolution, the end of the story.

Revise

Transitions Effective writers use transition words to move logically from one idea to another. Read the paragraph below. Then revise it and add transition words to improve the sentences.

The war seemed like it was never going to end. Andy wasn't happy that he wouldn't see his mom. He ate dinner with his grandmother. He ate peas and had an idea: "What if I send Mom drawings of what I've been doing with Grandma?"

____

____

____

____

____

____

____

Grammar Connection

Transitions and signal words help ideas flow from one sentence to the next and show the sequence of events. Some examples of transitions and signal words are *then, later on,* and *after many days.*

Revision Revise your draft, and check that you present plot events in a logical order, using a variety of transitions and signal words. Make sure that the sequence of events makes sense and won't confuse your readers.

kali9/E+/Getty Images

Peer Conferences

Review a Draft Listen carefully as a partner reads his or her work aloud. Take notes about what you liked and what was difficult to follow. Begin by telling what you liked about the draft. Ask questions that will help the writer think more about the writing. Make suggestions that you think will make the writing stronger and clearer. Use these sentence starters.

I liked your use of transitions because. . .

I have a question about. . .

This part of the story is unclear to me. Can you explain why. . . ?

Your draft could be clearer if you added. . .

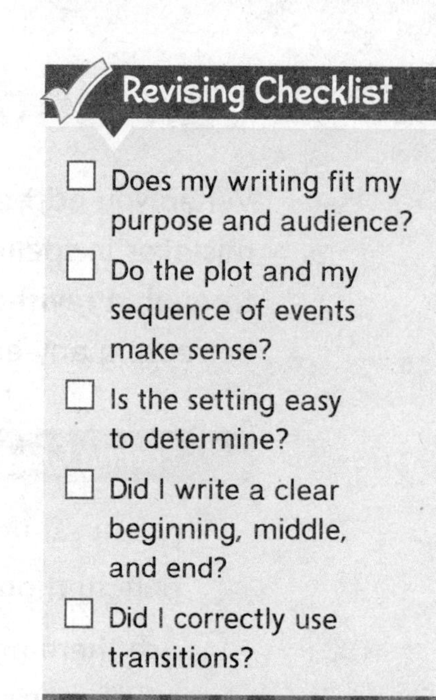

Partner Feedback After your partner gives you feedback on your draft, write one of the suggestions that you will use in your revision. Refer to the rubric on page 129 as you give feedback.

Based on my partner's feedback, I will ______________________________

____

____

____

After you finish giving each other feedback, reflect on the peer conference. What was helpful? What might you do differently next time?

Revision As you revise your draft, use the Revising Checklist to help you figure out what text you may need to move, elaborate on, or delete. Remember to use the rubric on page 129 to help you with your revision.

Edit and Proofread

When you **edit** and **proofread** your writing, you look for and correct mistakes in spelling, punctuation, capitalization, and grammar. Reading through a revised draft multiple times can help you make sure you're correcting any errors. Use the checklist below to edit your sentences.

Grammar Connections

As you proofread your story, make sure that you have capitalized historic events, proper names, and abbreviations such as *Mr.*, *Mrs.*, and *Dr.*

Editing Checklist

- ☐ Do all sentences begin with a capital letter and end with a punctuation mark?
- ☐ Are there any run-on sentences, sentence fragments, or sentences with incorrect subject-verb agreement?
- ☐ Are proper nouns capitalized?
- ☐ Are quotation marks used correctly?
- ☐ Are adverbs and descriptive adjectives used correctly?
- ☐ Are all words spelled correctly?

List two mistakes you found as you proofread your story.

1. ____

____

2. ____

____

Publish, Present, and Evaluate

Publishing When you **publish** your writing, you create a clean final copy that is free of mistakes. As you write your final draft be sure to write clearly in cursive. Check that you are holding your pencil or pen correctly.

Presentation When you are ready to **present** your work, rehearse your presentation. Use the Presenting Checklist to help you.

Evaluate After you publish your writing, use the rubric below to **evaluate** your writing.

What did you do successfully? ____________________

What needs more work? ____________________

____

Presenting Checklist

- ☐ Stand up straight.
- ☐ Look at the audience.
- ☐ Speak slowly and clearly.
- ☐ Speak loudly enough so that everyone can hear you.
- ☐ Answer questions thoughtfully.

4	3	2	1
• tells a story that takes place in the past and includes clear details about the plot and historical setting • sequence of events is logical and clear • uses a variety of signal and transition words and phrases	• tells a story that takes place in the past, but includes only a few details about the plot and historical setting • sequence of events mostly makes sense • uses some signal and transition words and phrases	• tells a story, but doesn't include details about the plot and setting • sequence of events is not completely logical • uses few signal and transition words and phrases	• story does not take place in the past and has no plot • sequence of events is not logical and is somewhat confusing • does not use signal or transition words and phrases

Talk About It

Essential Question

How are living things adapted to their environment?

Every living thing has developed a way to live in its environment. The photo shows an Australian lizard called a Thorny Devil. It has an adaptation that lets it get water from wherever it touches its body. Grooves on its body move water up to its mouth.

Talk with a partner about animals you know about and how they have adapted to their environments. Write your ideas in the web.

Adaptations

Spikes

hibernate

Go online to **my.mheducation.com** and read the "Blending In" Blast. Think about the different ways animals adapt to their ecosystems. How do these adaptations help the animals? Then blast back your response.

TAKE NOTES

To set a purpose for reading, look at the photo and read the caption and the title. Next, think about what you want to know. Write your purpose here and keep it in mind as your read.

As you read, make note of:

Interesting Words

Key Details

Mysterious Oceans

Essential Question

How are living things adapted to their environment?

Read about the adaptation of sea creatures to the deep ocean.

Crabs crawl among giant tube worms in the deep ocean. New ocean species are being discovered all the time.

Emory Kristof/National Geographic Stock

Deep Diving

It has no mouth, eyes, or stomach. Its soft body is encased in a white cylinder and topped with a red plume. It can grow to be eight feet tall. It is a sea creature known as a giant tube worm, and it lives without any sunlight on the deep, dark ocean floor.

What we sometimes call the deep ocean, in contrast to shallow waters, covers almost two-thirds of Earth's surface. On average, oceans are about two miles deep. However, the deepest point known on Earth, Challenger Deep, descends nearly seven miles.

The ocean's floor is varied, consisting of vast plains, steep canyons, and towering mountains. It includes active, **dormant,** and extinct volcanoes. This undersea world is a harsh environment because of its **frigid** temperatures and lack of sunshine.

The deep ocean is also a mysterious environment that remains largely unexplored. Little is known about it or its creatures. Do any of them **cache** food the way land animals do? Do any ocean species **hibernate?** As one example among countless mysteries, not a single, live giant squid had ever been spotted until a few years ago. We knew they existed only because their corpses had been found.

The Challenger Deep is located in an undersea canyon called the Mariana Trench.

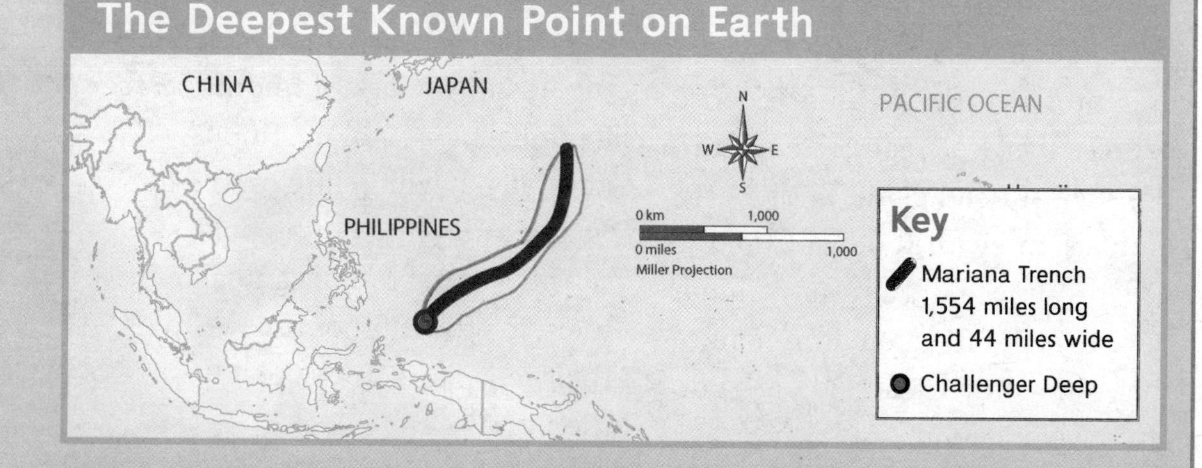

EXPOSITORY TEXT

FIND TEXT EVIDENCE

Read

Paragraphs 1-2

Ask and Answer Questions

What is a question you can ask and answer about the ocean? Write the question and underline the answer.

Paragraphs 3-4

Cause and Effect

Circle the text that tells why the deep ocean is a harsh environment.

Map

Look at the map. In what ocean is the Mariana Trench located?

Reread

Author's Craft

Why do you think the author begins the text by describing a sea creature?

SHARED READ

FIND TEXT EVIDENCE

Read

Paragraphs 1-3

Cause and Effect

What allowed scientists to begin exploring the deep ocean floor?

Draw a box around the effect of this exploration.

Paragraph 4

Context Clues

How do context clues help you to determine the meaning of *bioluminus*?

Reread

Author's Craft

How do the photographs and captions support the text? What do they help you understand?

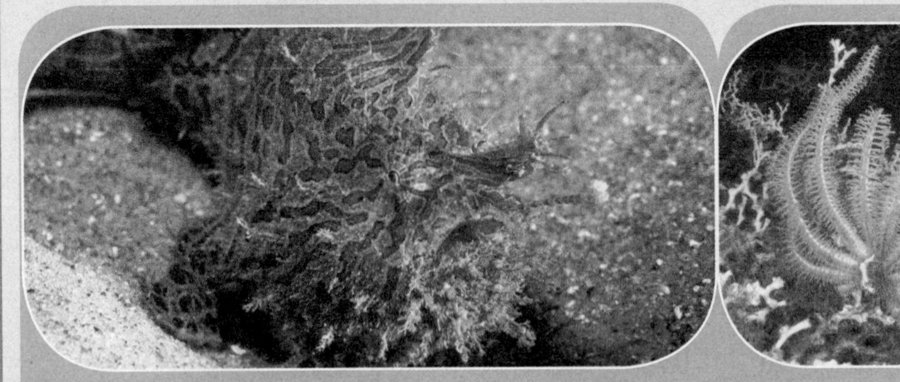

This fish, the striated frogfish, lures prey. The nose is an adaptation to life in the deep ocean.

A basket starfish rests in a deep-sea coral reef.

Amazing Adaptations

When a submersible, or submarine, was invented that could descend farther than any other craft, scientists were then able to make the odyssey to the deep ocean floor. However, exploration remains difficult, and they have since seen merely five percent of the underwater world.

As scientists anticipated, life generally seems sparse at the bottom of the deep ocean. Few creatures can survive there. Food sources that sea creatures depend on, such as dead plants and animals, rarely drift down from the ocean's surface. As a result, animals have to adapt to an environment that is not only frigid and dark but also has little food.

One example of an **adaptation** to this environment is seen in the starfish. Deep sea starfish grow larger and more aggressive than their shallow water relatives. They can't afford to wait for an occasional snail to pass by. Instead, deep sea starfish are predators that actively **forage** for food. They reach up their five arms, which have pincers at the ends, to catch meals of **agile**, fast-moving shrimp.

Anglerfish also are adapted to the herculean task of finding scarce food. Each has a bioluminous, or naturally glowing, lure on the top of its head. This shining pole is sensitive to vibrations and allows them to attract other fish. With their huge jaws, they quickly seize their prey.

Heated Habitats

What has truly surprised scientists, however, is the discovery of another, very different type of environment on the deep ocean floor. They found that cracks, or vents, in Earth's surface exist underwater, just as they do on dry land. Sea water rushes into these vents, where it mingles with chemicals. The water is also heated by magma, or hot melted rock. When the water from the vent bursts back into the ocean, it creates geysers and hot springs.

To scientists' amazement, the habitats around these vents teem with life. In addition to tube worms, there are huge clams, eyeless shrimp, crabs, and mussels, along with many kinds of bacteria. One odd creature is the Pompeii worm. It has a fleece of bacteria on its back that, as far as scientists can determine, **insulates** it from heat.

How can so much life exist where there is so little food or sunlight? Scientists have discovered that many creatures transform the chemicals from the vents into food. The process is called chemosynthesis. Because of this process, animals are able to flourish in these remarkable habitats. Creatures that don't use chemosynthesis for food, such as crabs, eat the ones that do.

There are many mysteries to be found and solved at the bottom of the deep sea. In the last few decades alone, scientists have discovered more than 1,500 ocean species! If scientists continue sea exploration, they are bound to discover many more.

Summarize

Use your notes to orally summarize the most important ideas you learned about the deep sea in "Mysterious Oceans."

EXPOSITORY TEXT

FIND TEXT EVIDENCE

Read

Paragraphs 1-4

Ask and Answer Questions

What is a question you can ask and answer to check your comprehension of this section? Underline the answer to your question.

____

____

____

Reread

Author's Craft

How does the author help you visualize life around the vents in the deep ocean?

Fluency

Take turns reading aloud the third paragraph on page 135. Talk about how using an appropriate rate helps you focus on reading scientific terms with accuracy.

Vocabulary

Use the example sentences to talk with a partner about each word. Then answer the questions.

adaptation

Changing color is an **adaptation** some lizards have made to their environments.

How is fur an example of an adaptation?

____

____

agile

Kim was such an **agile** gymnast, she could do a back bend on a balance beam.

Why should athletes be agile?

____

____

cache

My parents **cache** jewelry and other treasures in a box in our basement.

Where else might people cache special things?

____

____

dormant

The guide explained that the volcano was **dormant**, so we felt safe standing near it.

Why is it safe to visit a dormant volcano?

____

____

forage

When winter comes, elk, deer, and other animals often must **forage** for food.

Why is it hard to forage for food during winter?

____

____

Build Your Word List Reread the first paragraph on page 134. Circle the word *invented*. In your writer's notebook, use a word web to write more forms of the word. For example, *inventor*. Use an online or print dictionary to find more words that are related.

frigid

We drank a hot beverage to warm up after being outside on a **frigid** day.

Do you usually wear shorts in frigid weather?

____

____

____

hibernate

Some animals, such as the dormouse, **hibernate** during the winter.

Why do some animals hibernate in the winter?

____

____

____

insulates

My coat **insulates** my body against the cold.

What insulates a cat against the cold?

____

____

____

Context Clues

If you read an unfamiliar or multiple-meaning word, you can look for clues to its meaning in the paragraph in which it appears.

FIND TEXT EVIDENCE

In the first paragraph of "Mysterious Oceans" on page 133, I see the word cylinder. *I'm not sure what* cylinder *means. Since the creature being discussed is called a tube worm, I think a cylinder may refer to the tube around the worm.*

Its soft body is encased in a white cylinder and topped with a red plume. It can grow to be eight feet tall. It is a sea creature known as a giant tube worm, and it lives without any sunlight on the deep, dark ocean floor.

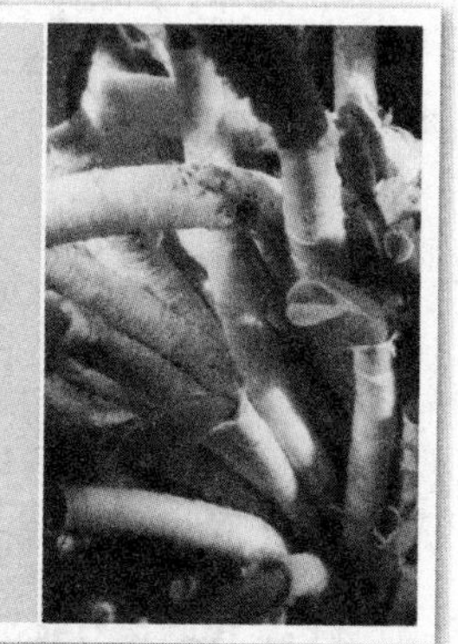

Your Turn Use context clues to find the meaning of these words in "Mysterious Oceans."

sparse, *page 134* ______________________________

____

aggressive, *page 134* ______________________________

____

Emory Kristof/National Geographic Stock

Reread | SHARED READ

Ask and Answer Questions

Asking and answering questions can help you monitor your comprehension of complex scientific text. This can also help deepen your understanding of the topic. You can ask yourself what the main ideas are or reasons for a statement. You can reread parts of the text to find the answers and deepen your understanding.

Quick Tip

Begin the questions you ask yourself with these words:

Who ______?

What ______?

Where ______?

When ______?

Why ______?

How ______?

FIND TEXT EVIDENCE

The last paragraph in the section "Deep Diving" on page 133 of "Mysterious Oceans" asks several questions about oceans. You may wonder why these questions are being asked.

Page 133

The deep ocean is also a mysterious environment that remains largely unexplored. Little is known about it or its creatures. Do any of them **cache** food the way land animals do? Do any ocean species **hibernate**? As one example among countless mysteries, not a single, live giant squid had ever been spotted until a few years ago. We knew they existed only because their corpses had been found.

There must be reasons why we know so little about ocean life. I'm going to ask myself, "Why is the deep ocean so mysterious?" I will reread the section to try to answer this question.

Your Turn Use the information in the first two paragraphs of "Deep Diving" on page 133 to answer the question "Why is the deep ocean so mysterious?"

______

______

______

______

Maps

The selection "Mysterious Ocean" is expository text. Expository text presents information about a topic, with main ideas and key details. It may be organized to show cause-and-effect relationships. The authors of expository text may include text features such as photos, captions, and maps.

Quick Tip

The title of a map identifies, or tells, its topic. Always read the title first. Then study the map and think about how it relates, or connects, to the topic.

FIND TEXT EVIDENCE

I can tell "Mysterious Oceans" is expository text. The text gives information about oceans and includes main ideas and cause-and-effect relationships. A map gives visual information.

Page 133

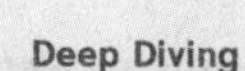

Deep Diving

It has no mouth, eyes, or stomach. Its soft body is encased in a white cylinder and topped with a red plume. It can grow to be eight feet tall. It is a sea creature known as a giant tube worm, and it lives without any sunlight on the deep, dark ocean floor.

What we sometimes call the deep ocean, in contrast to shallow waters, covers almost two-thirds of Earth's surface. On average, oceans are about two miles deep. However, the deepest point known on Earth, Challenger Deep, descends nearly seven miles.

The ocean's floor is **varied**, consisting of vast plains, steep canyons, and towering mountains. It includes active, **dormant**, and extinct volcanoes. This undersea world is a harsh environment because of its **frigid** temperatures and lack of sunshine.

The deep ocean is also a mysterious environment that remains largely unexplored. Little is known about it or its creatures. Do any of them **cache** food the way land animals do? Do any ocean species **hibernate?** As one example among countless mysteries, not a single, live giant squid had ever been spotted until a few years ago. We knew they existed only because their corpses had been found.

The Challenger Deep is located in an undersea canyon called the Mariana Trench.

The Deepest Known Point on Earth

Map

A map is a flat picture of an area. Most maps have a title, a scale to show how many miles are represented, a compass rose to show directions, and a key that explains colors or symbols.

Your Turn Study the map on page 133. What is the approximate length and width of the Mariana Trench? How does the map help you visualize it?

____

____

____

Cause and Effect

To figure out cause-and-effect relationships in a text, first look for an event or action that makes something happen. This is the **cause**. Then look for what happens as a result of that cause. This is the **effect**. Words and phrases such as *because of, as a result, if/then,* or *when* can signal cause and effect.

FIND TEXT EVIDENCE

In the first paragraph of the section "Amazing Adaptations" on page 134 of "Mysterious Oceans," the author explains that a new type of submersible was invented. The word when *signals a cause-and-effect relationship. This invention caused something else to happen.*

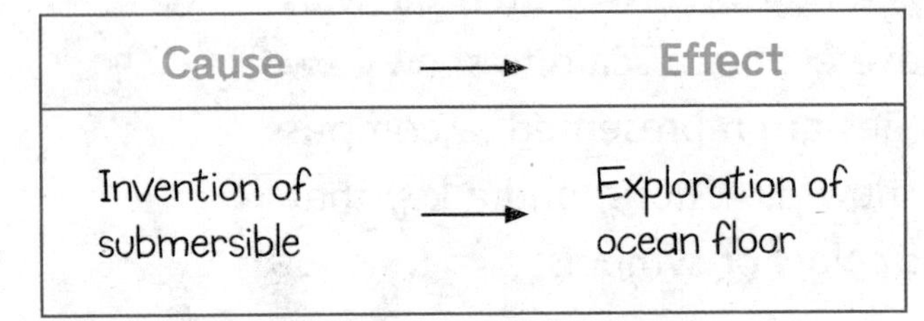

Cause	→	Effect
Invention of submersible	→	Exploration of ocean floor

Your Turn Reread the rest of the section "Amazing Adaptations" on page 134. Identify the cause-and-effect relationships explained in these paragraphs and list them in your graphic organizer on page 141.

Quick Tip

To identify cause-and effect-relationships, ask yourself these questions:

What happened?

Why did it happen?

The answer to *Why did it happen?* is the cause.

The answer to *What happened?* is the effect.

Cause	→	Effect
	→	
	→	
	→	
	→	

Respond to Reading

Discuss the prompt below. Think about how the author presents the information. Use your notes and graphic organizer.

How does the author help you understand how sea creatures have adapted to life in the deep ocean?

Quick Tip

Use these sentence starters to discuss the text and to organize ideas.

- *The author uses a cause-and-effect text structure to explain. . .*
- *The author describes. . .*
- *The photos and captions help. . .*

Grammar Connections

As you write your response, use transition words and phrases to connect your ideas. Some transitions are *such as, then, however, for example, in fact, also.*

Photo Research

Photo research for a presentation is easiest to do online. Detailed and colorful photos will support your topic and ideas. They can also make your presentation more interesting. As you look for appropriate photos, think about the following questions:

- Have I narrowed my search so I can quickly find good photos?
- Is the website reliable?
- Do the photos accurately show what I want to say?

What else would you need to think about when developing a plan to do photo research?

Create a Slideshow With a partner or group, research photos of animals with interesting adaptations. Then create a multimodal slideshow to present what you find. A slideshow is multimodal because you can present information in more than one way. For example, in addition to the photographs, you can use sound effects, music, and text. Remember to keep track of your sources. Use these questions when preparing information to go with your photos:

- Where do the animals live?
- How do the adaptations help the animals survive?
- How are the adaptations of the animals the same or different?

Discuss the websites you might use for your research. After you complete your slideshow, you will demonstrate your understanding of the information you gathered by presenting your work to your class.

The desert fox lives in a hot environment. Its large ears help to release heat to keep the body cool.

The photo and caption above show an example of an animal adaptation.

Tech Tip

If you are having problems finding appropriate photos, try using different key words.

Reread | ANCHOR TEXT

Literature Anthology: pages 450–465

Survival at 40 Below

How does the author feel about the wood frog's adaptations to the cold?

Talk About It Reread **Literature Anthology** page 453. Turn to your partner and discuss how the author talks about how frogs change in order to survive the Arctic.

Cite Text Evidence How does the author help you understand how she feels about how the frog adapts to the Arctic? Write text evidence.

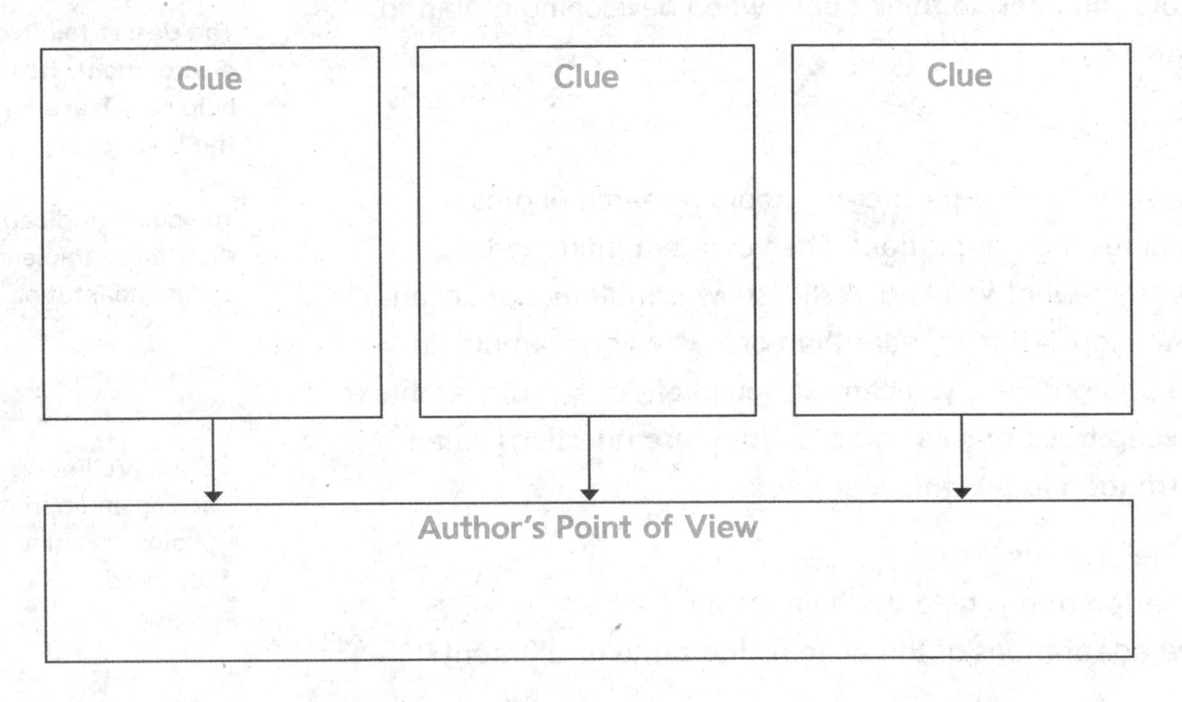

Write The author thinks that ______________________________

____

____

Make Inferences

You can often infer how the author feels about a subject by paying attention to the author's word choice. Think about the words the author uses to describe the wood frog and what it does. Are they words that give a positive feeling or a negative feeling? Based on her word choice, what inferences can you make about the author's feelings toward the wood frog?

Why does the author describe the arctic fox as an acrobat?

Talk About It Reread **Literature Anthology** page 457. Notice that the author uses the simile "like" to compare the arctic fox and an acrobat. Turn to your partner and discuss how the arctic fox is like an acrobat and how it is not.

Cite Text Evidence How are the arctic fox and an acrobat alike and different? Write text evidence in the diagram.

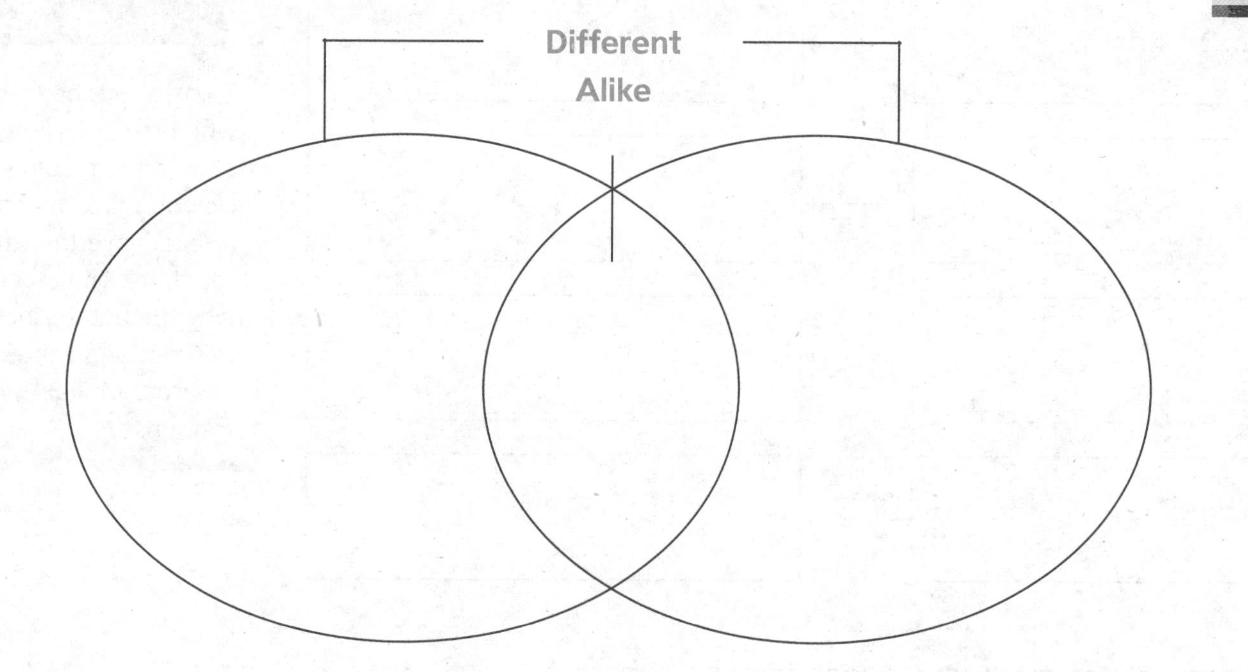

Write The author describes the arctic fox as an acrobat ______

______

______

______

Quick Tip

Use these sentence starters to talk about the text and to help you fill in the Venn diagram.

- *The fox is similar to an acrobat because. . .*
- *A fox is different than an acrobat because. . .*

Reread | ANCHOR TEXT

How does the author use sensory language to paint a picture with words on page 463?

Talk About It Reread **Literature Anthology** page 463. Turn to a partner and talk about what the Arctic is like at the beginning of spring.

Cite Text Evidence What words and phrases help you picture what spring is like in the Arctic? Write text evidence.

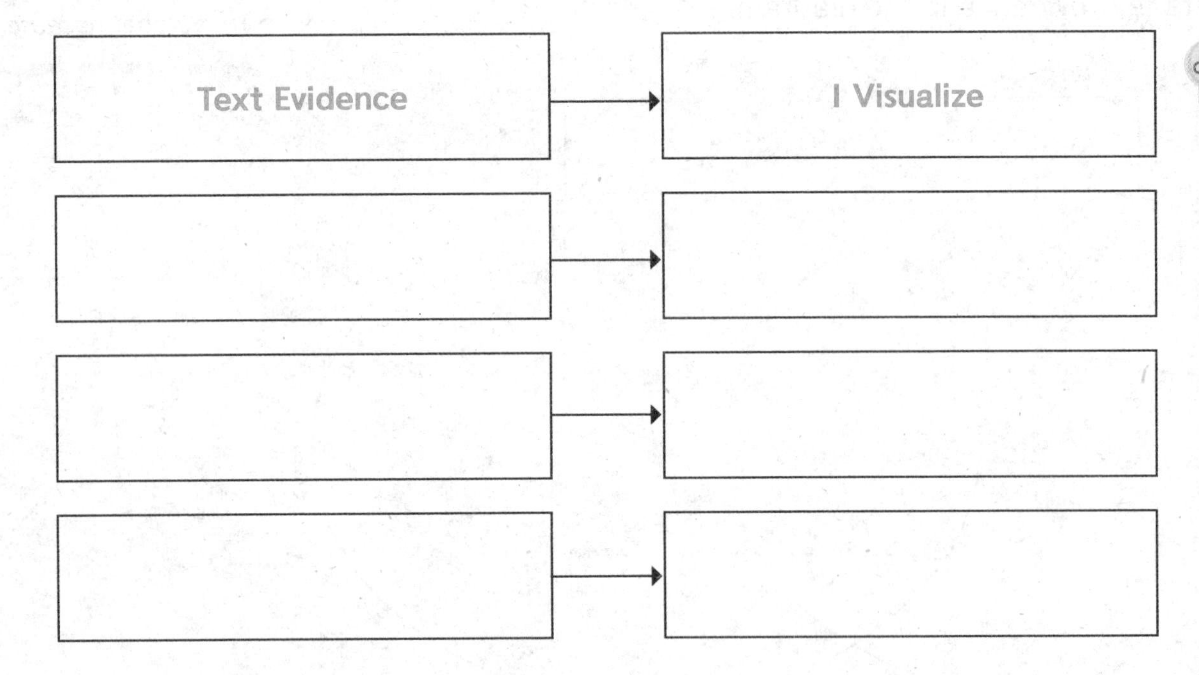

Write The author uses sensory language to paint a picture ________________

____

____

____

____

Quick Tip

Pay close attention to the illustration. Use it along with the written text to help you create mental images of the beginning of spring in the Arctic.

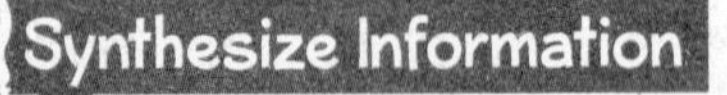

Synthesize Information

Think about how you feel when spring emerges after a long, cold winter. Do you think animals and insects have the same reaction? Then, consider why the author includes a description of the woolly bear caterpillar basking in the sun.

Respond to Reading

Discuss the prompt below. Apply your own knowledge of animals, especially those that live in cold environments, to inform your answer. Use your notes and graphic organizer.

How does the author express her point of view about the animals that live and adapt to the Arctic environment?

Quick Tip

Use these sentence starters to talk about and cite text evidence.

- *The author uses words and phrases to help me understand . . .*
- *She uses figurative language to compare . . .*
- *I know how she feels about animals because . . .*

Self-Selected Reading

Choose a text and fill in your writer's notebook with the title, author, and genre. Record your purpose for reading. For example, you may be reading to answer a question or for entertainment.

USFWS/Donna Dewhurst

Reread | PAIRED SELECTION

Why the Evergreen Trees Never Lose Their Leaves

1 "No, indeed," answered the birch-tree, drawing her fair leaves away. "We of the great forest have our own birds to help. I can do nothing for you."

2 "The birch is not very strong," said the little bird to itself, "and it might be that she could not hold me easily. I will ask the oak." So the bird said, "Great oak-tree, you are so strong, will you not let me live on your boughs till my friends come back in the springtime?"

3 "In the springtime!" cried the oak. "That is a long way off. How do I know what you might do in all that time? Birds are always looking for something to eat, and you might even eat up some of my acorns."

Literature Anthology
pages 468–471

Reread the excerpt. **Circle** the lines of dialogue that tell you something about the trees' characters. Write what it reveals about the trees.

____

____

Talk with a partner about what you can infer about the little bird from his reaction to the birch tree. **Underline** the words in paragraph 2 that tell you his reaction.

1 "Come right here, then," said the friendly spruce-tree, for it was her voice that had called. "You shall live on my warmest branch all winter if you choose."

2 "Will you really let me?" asked the little bird eagerly.

3 "Indeed, I will," answered the kind-hearted spruce-tree. "If your friends have flown away, it is time for the trees to help you. Here is the branch where my leaves are thickest and softest."

4 "My branches are not very thick," said the friendly pine-tree, "but I am big and strong, and I can keep the north wind from you and the spruce."

5 "I can help too," said a little juniper-tree. "I can give you berries all winter long, and every bird knows that juniper berries are good."

Reread the excerpt. **Underline** the sentence in paragraph 1 that tells what the spruce-tree offers the little bird.

Underline the sentence in paragraph 5 that tells what the juniper-tree offers the little bird.

Talk about the trees with a partner. How do they respond to the bird? **Circle** words that show what the trees are like.

What do these trees do? Use text evidence to support your response.

____

____

____

____

____

Reread | PAIRED SELECTION

Why does the author contrast the behavior of the two groups of trees?

Talk About It Reread the excerpts on pages 148 and 149. With a partner, discuss the different groups of trees. How are they different?

Cite Text Evidence What words and phrases describe the behavior of the two groups of trees? Write what it tells you about the trees.

Text Evidence	→	What It Tells
	→	
	→	
	→	
	→	

Write The author shows the two groups of trees differently because ______

______

______

______

Quick Tip

As you reread, think about what the behavior of each tree means. Take notes on a piece of paper. Use your notes to help you fill in the chart.

Point of View

Point of view can mean the perspective from which a story is told. In first-person point of view, the story is told from the perspective of a character who is also the narrator. In third-person point of view, the narrator is not in the story. In third-person limited, the narrator knows the thoughts and feelings of only one character. In third-person omniscient, or all knowing, the narrator knows the thoughts and feelings of all the characters.

Readers to Writers

If you choose to write from a third-person limited point of view, the narrator will tell the thoughts and feelings of only one character. Other characters may say how they feel or express a thought through dialogue. In a first-person point of view, the narrator takes part in the actions of the story and refers to himself or herself as *I*.

FIND TEXT EVIDENCE

In "Why the Evergreen Trees Never Lose Their Leaves," the author tells the story in third-person limited, focusing on the little bird. In paragraph 2 on page 148, the words "said the little bird to itself" show that the narrator knows the bird's thoughts and feelings.

> "The birch is not very strong," said the little bird to itself, "and it might be that she could not hold me easily. I will ask the oak."

Your Turn Reread paragraphs 1 and 2 on page 148.

- How do you know the point of view is third-person limited?

____

____

- How might the story have changed if told from other points of view?

____

____

Integrate | MAKE CONNECTIONS

Text Connections

How are the adaptations you see in this photograph similar to the adaptations described in *Survival at 40 Below* and "Why the Evergreen Trees Never Lose Their Leaves"?

Talk About It Look at the photograph and read the caption. With a partner, talk about what you see and how this animal has adapted to its habitat.

Cite Text Evidence **Draw a box** around details that help show the setting of the photograph. **Circle** the hare's adaptations. **Underline** evidence in the caption that tells more about how this animal adapts. Think about how these adaptations help the hare survive.

Write The adaptations in this photograph are similar to the ones in the selections because ______

______

______

______

______

______

______

______

Quick Tip

Look back at the two texts in the question and list the adaptations described in them. Then, compare those adaptations to the ones in the photograph.

Can you see this snowshoe hare? His fur turns white in winter. During summer months, this animal is brown. It takes 10 weeks for its fur to change completely.

Present Your Work

Discuss how you will present your multimedia slideshow of animals with interesting adaptations. Use the Presenting Checklist as you practice your presentation. Discuss the sentence starters below and write your answers.

After researching unique animal adaptations, I realized ______________________

____

____

____

I would like to know more about ______________________

____

____

____

Tech Tip

Listen to the audio, or sound, portion of your presentation to make sure that people in different parts of the room can clearly hear it. Adjust the volume as needed before you present.

Presenting Checklist

- ☐ Rehearse your presentation with your partner or group. Make sure you have the correct information for each slide.
- ☐ Make sure everyone in the group has a role in the presentation.
- ☐ Make eye contact with your audience.
- ☐ Make sure that everyone in your audience can see and hear your presentation.
- ☐ Listen carefully to questions. Then provide complete answers.

Talk About It

Essential Question

What can our connections to the world teach us?

As we go out into the world, we find ways to stay connected to our friends, families, and countries. Staying connected helps us to feel that we are part of the larger world.

Look at the photo. What is the boy doing? How is he staying connected to his family, friends, and the world as he sits within sight of the famous Taj Mahal in India? Talk with a partner about how people stay connected to people and places. Write your ideas in the web.

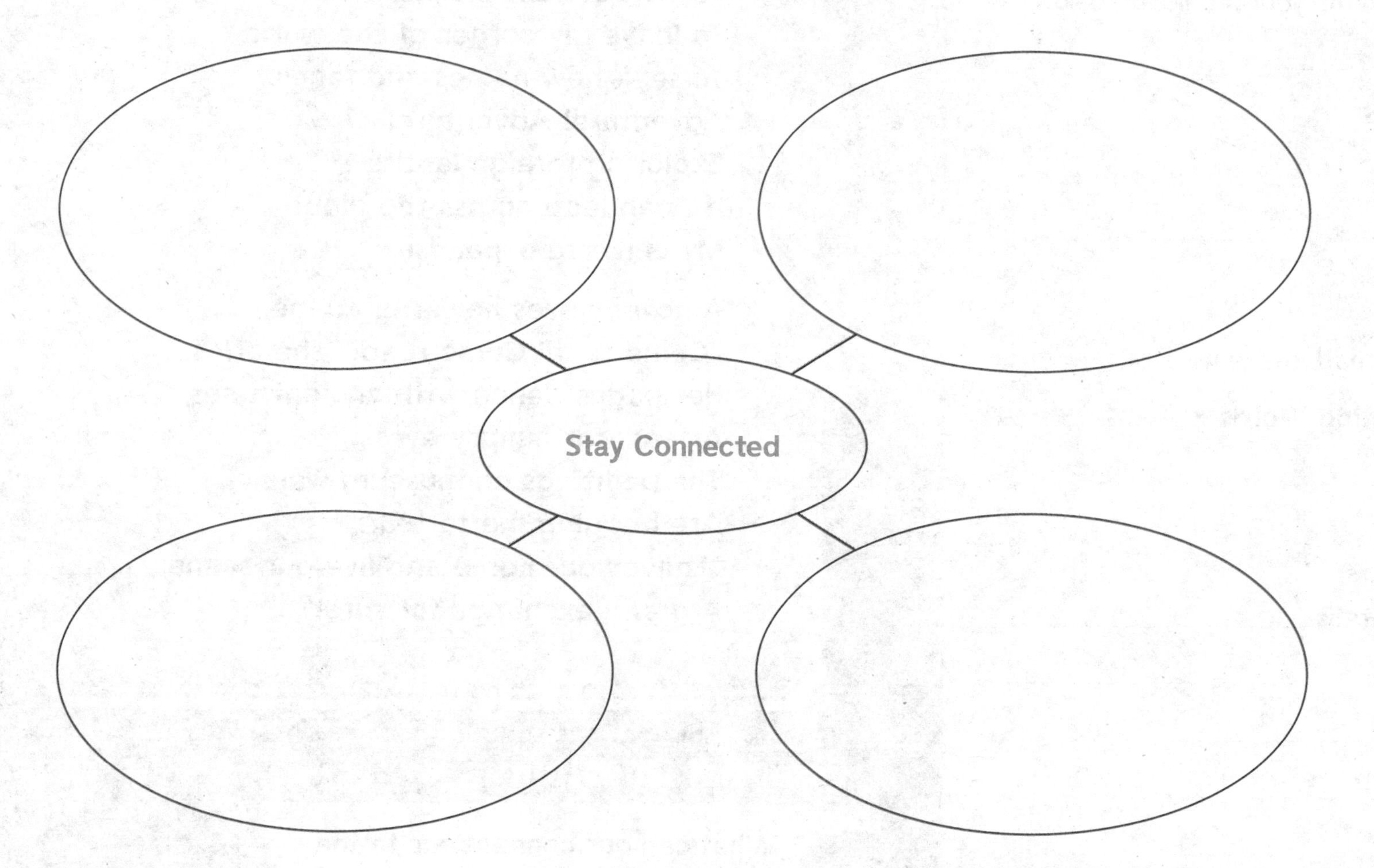

Go online to **my.mheducation.com** and read the "Be Nice" Blast. Think about how being nice helps people to get along. Then blast back your response.

Purepix/Alamy Stock Photo

SHARED READ

TAKE NOTES

Preview the poems by looking at the photos and reading the titles. Predict what you think each poem will be about. Write your prediction below.

____

As you read, make note of:

Interesting Words ____________________________

Key Details ____________________________

To Travel!

To travel! To travel!
To visit distant places;
To leave my corner of the world
To seek new names and faces.
Adventure! Adventure!
Exploring foreign lands;
If I can leap across the globe,
My universe expands!

A novel waves her arms to me,
"Come read! Come read!" she cries.
Her pages dance with ancient tales,
A feast for hungry eyes!
The paintings on museum walls
Are begging me to tour:
"Leave your home and live our scenes,
A grand exchange for sure!"

Essential Question

What can our connections to the world teach us?

Read two poems about connecting with other cultures and with nature.

To travel! To travel!
Through timeless books and art,
I enter and experience
A life so far apart.

I sail across the seven seas,
My heart soars like a bird.
And soon I'm hearing languages
I've never, ever heard.

Far across the seven seas,
Aromas fill the air.
Foods I've never, ever tried
Are eaten everywhere!
Music blares a different tune,
And strange, new clothes are worn.
Parents pass on customs
To the young ones who are born.

I've traveled! I've traveled!
It's left me more aware;
A valuable connection
To the universe we share.
By reading books and viewing art,
I've learned a thing or two:
The world was made not just for me,
But made for me and you!

— Jad Abbas

FIND TEXT EVIDENCE

Read

Page 156

Personification

Circle text in the second stanza that describes what the paintings want the speaker to do. What does this help you to know?

Pages 156–157

Make Inferences

What does the speaker think of reading books and viewing art?

Reread

Author's Craft

How does the poet use simile, a comparison using *like* or *as*, to show the speaker's feelings?

SHARED READ

FIND TEXT EVIDENCE

Read

Page 158

Assonance and Consonance

Circle four words in the third line that show assonance, or the repetition of the same vowel sound in two or more words. What feelings do the sounds contribute to the poem?

____

Page 158

Point of View

Underline a key detail that tells you the speaker's point of view about what her grandmother is doing. What is the speaker's point of view?

____

____

Reread

Author's Craft

What can you infer about the speaker from the last two sentences on this page? What words and phrases helped you make your inference?

Wild Blossoms

One bright summer morning, my grandmother asked me to help her plant some flowers. I pedaled my bike downtown, wheels weaving between sunbeams. In the sky, clouds exchanged greetings, their language inaudible, while I, on my errand, brought a long list of seeds to the store. Back on my bike, I followed the same sensible route I always took to Grandmother's house. I watched with surprise as she tore off the tops of the seed packets and shook them willy-nilly around the backyard, then told me to do the same.

John Robertson/Alamy Stock Photo

"I thought we were planting a garden," I told her,
"with row after row of flowers." She said, "Oh, no!
I prefer a mountain meadow, one with plenty
of variety." As she talked, bees buzzed about
in excitable flight, impatient for blossoms.
Quick swifts and happy sparrows dipped, dove, and darted
after the falling seeds. My grandmother and I
danced about the backyard, arms outstretched, letting seeds
loose on the wind, joyfully dreaming of the wild
beauty that would fill the yard, and us, all summer.

— Amelia Campos

Make Connections

How do the connections described in the poems compare with your own experiences?

Talk about whether your prediction on page 156 was correct.

FIND TEXT EVIDENCE

Read

Pages 158–159

Narrative Poetry

How do you know this is a narrative poem, one that tells a story?

____

____

____

Page 159

Point of View

By the end of the poem, what is the speaker's point of view about how her grandmother plants a garden?

____

____

Underline the details that helped you find your answer.

Reread

Author's Craft

Look at the third and fourth sentences on this page. How does the poet's use of imagery help you visualize what the speaker is seeing?

Vocabulary

Use the example sentences to talk with a partner about each word. Then answer the questions.

blares

When a trumpet **blares,** Frankie covers his ears.

What might be the reason why someone blares music?

connection

Ron feels a strong **connection** to the players on his soccer team.

How would you establish a connection with a new friend?

errand

My mom sent me on an **errand** to mail a letter.

What errand would you do for a friend or a relative?

exchange

Milo and his brothers were paid ten dollars in **exchange** for shoveling snow.

What favor might you do in exchange for free movie tickets?

Poetry Terms

personification

Poets use **personification** to make objects, animals, or ideas resemble people.

How might personification help describe a thunderstorm?

assonance

A poem using **assonance** includes words with the same vowel sound.

List three words that have assonance with the word *moon*.

consonance

A poem with **consonance** has words with the same middle or final consonant sound.

Name three words that have consonance with the word *home.*

____

____

imagery

With **imagery**, poets use words to create a vivid picture.

What imagery might you use to describe a rainy day?

____

____

____

Build Your Word List Pick a word you found interesting in either poem. Look up the word's meaning and origin, or the language it comes from, in a print or online dictionary. Write the word and its meaning and origin in your writer's notebook.

Personification

Personification is a type of figurative language. **Personification** is the use of human characteristics to describe nonhuman things, such as animals, objects, or ideas. Poets use personification to create vivid images and to help the reader picture a detail or understand an idea.

FIND TEXT EVIDENCE

In "To Travel!" a novel is described as a person waving her arms and crying, "Come read!" The pages "dance" and eyes are described as "hungry." These human descriptions make books and their contents seem exciting and alive for the reader.

A novel waves her arms to me,
"Come read! Come read!" she cries.
Her pages dance with ancient tales,
A feast for hungry eyes!

Your Turn How is personification used to describe clouds in "Wild Blossoms"? What is the effect of this?

____

____

____

Assonance and Consonance

Poets may repeat sounds in words for emphasis or effect. **Assonance** is the repetition of the same vowel sound in two or more words. **Consonance** is the repetition of a final or middle consonant sound. The sounds contribute to a poem's feeling.

Quick Tip

If you are unsure if a vowel is making a long sound, look the word up in a dictionary. A line above a vowel means it has a long sound. This means the letter sounds like its name. For example, ā as in *pāge*.

FIND TEXT EVIDENCE

Reread the poem "To Travel!" on pages 156 and 157. Look for examples of assonance and consonance.

Page 156

A novel waves her arms to me,
"Come read! Come read!" she cries.
Her pages dance with ancient tales,
A feast for hungry eyes!
The paintings on museum walls
Are begging me to tour:
"Leave your home and live our scenes,
A grand exchange for sure!"

The long a sound in pages, ancient, *and* tales *is repeated to emphasize the contents of the novel. The repetition of the /z/ sound in the words* pages, tales, eyes, paintings, museum, walls, *and* scenes, *creates a feeling of how much there is to see and do.*

Your Turn Find examples of assonance and consonance in "Wild Blossoms," on page 159. Say the words in those lines aloud. What feelings do the sounds contribute to the poem?

____

____

____

____

Lyric and Narrative

Lyric poetry expresses personal thoughts and feelings. It has a musical quality and may include rhyme and rhythm. It often contains imagery.

Narrative poetry tells a story and sometimes has characters and dialogue. It may have meter and often contains imagery.

Readers to Writers

When you write about a poem, remember to distinguish between the poet and the speaker. The poet is the author of the poem. The speaker is the narrator or voice telling the poem.

FIND TEXT EVIDENCE

I can tell that "To Travel!" is a lyric poem expressing the speaker's personal feelings. "Wild Blossoms" is a narrative poem that tells a story. Both poems contain imagery, or words that help readers create mental images and deepen their understanding.

Page 157

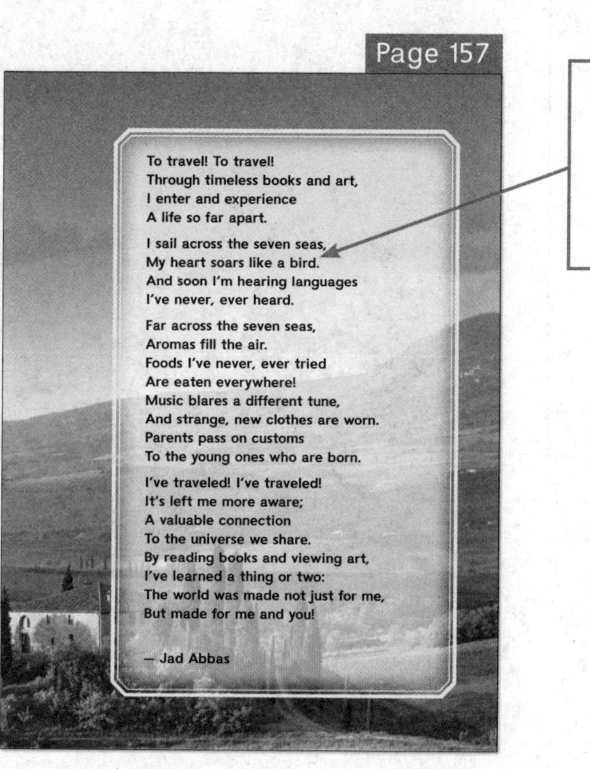

To travel! To travel!
Through timeless books and art,
I enter and experience
A life so far apart.

I sail across the seven seas,
My heart soars like a bird.
And soon I'm hearing languages
I've never, ever heard.

Far across the seven seas,
Aromas fill the air.
Foods I've never, ever tried
Are eaten everywhere!
Music blares a different tune,
And strange, new clothes are worn.
Parents pass on customs
To the young ones who are born.

I've traveled! I've traveled!
It's left me more aware;
A valuable connection
To the universe we share.
By reading books and viewing art,
I've learned a thing or two:
The world was made not just for me,
But made for me and you!

— Jad Abbas

"To Travel!" is a lyric poem. The line *My heart soars like a bird* expresses the speaker's feelings about traveling the world. The line *I sail across the seven seas* shows imagery of traveling.

Your Turn Compare the way the speakers of "To Travel!" and "Wild Blossoms" express themselves. How are the poems similar and different?

____

____

____

____

____

Point of View

The **point of view** is the individual way the speaker of the poem thinks. Details such as word choice and the thoughts expressed are clues to the speaker's point of view.

FIND TEXT EVIDENCE

"To Travel!" and "Wild Blossoms" are written in the first person, and they express individual points of view. I'll reread "To Travel!" to look for key details that help me figure out the speaker's point of view.

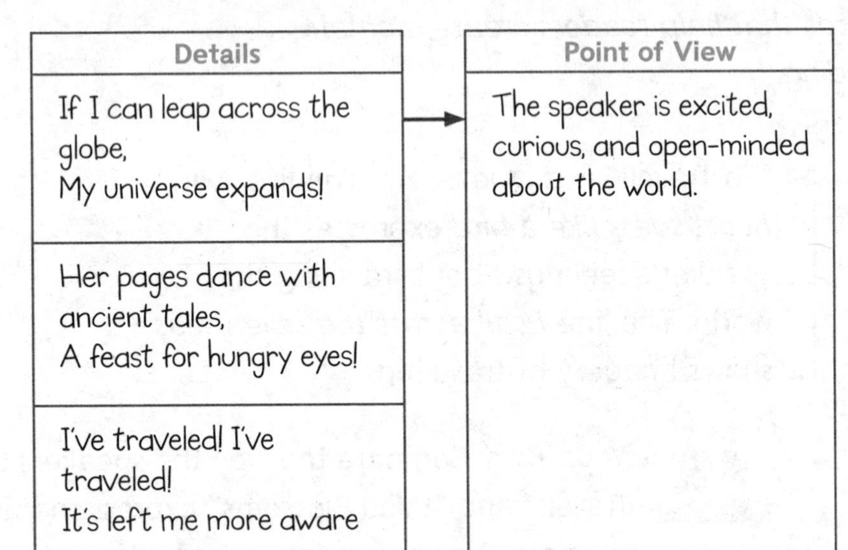

Details	Point of View
If I can leap across the globe, My universe expands!	The speaker is excited, curious, and open-minded about the world.
Her pages dance with ancient tales, A feast for hungry eyes!	
I've traveled! I've traveled! It's left me more aware	

Your Turn Reread the poem "Wild Blossoms." List key details in the graphic organizer on page 165. Use the details to figure out the speaker's point of view.

Quick Tip

As you reread "Wild Blossoms," look for sentences that are written in the first person, or where the pronoun "I" is used. Think about how these sentences reveal the speaker's point of view.

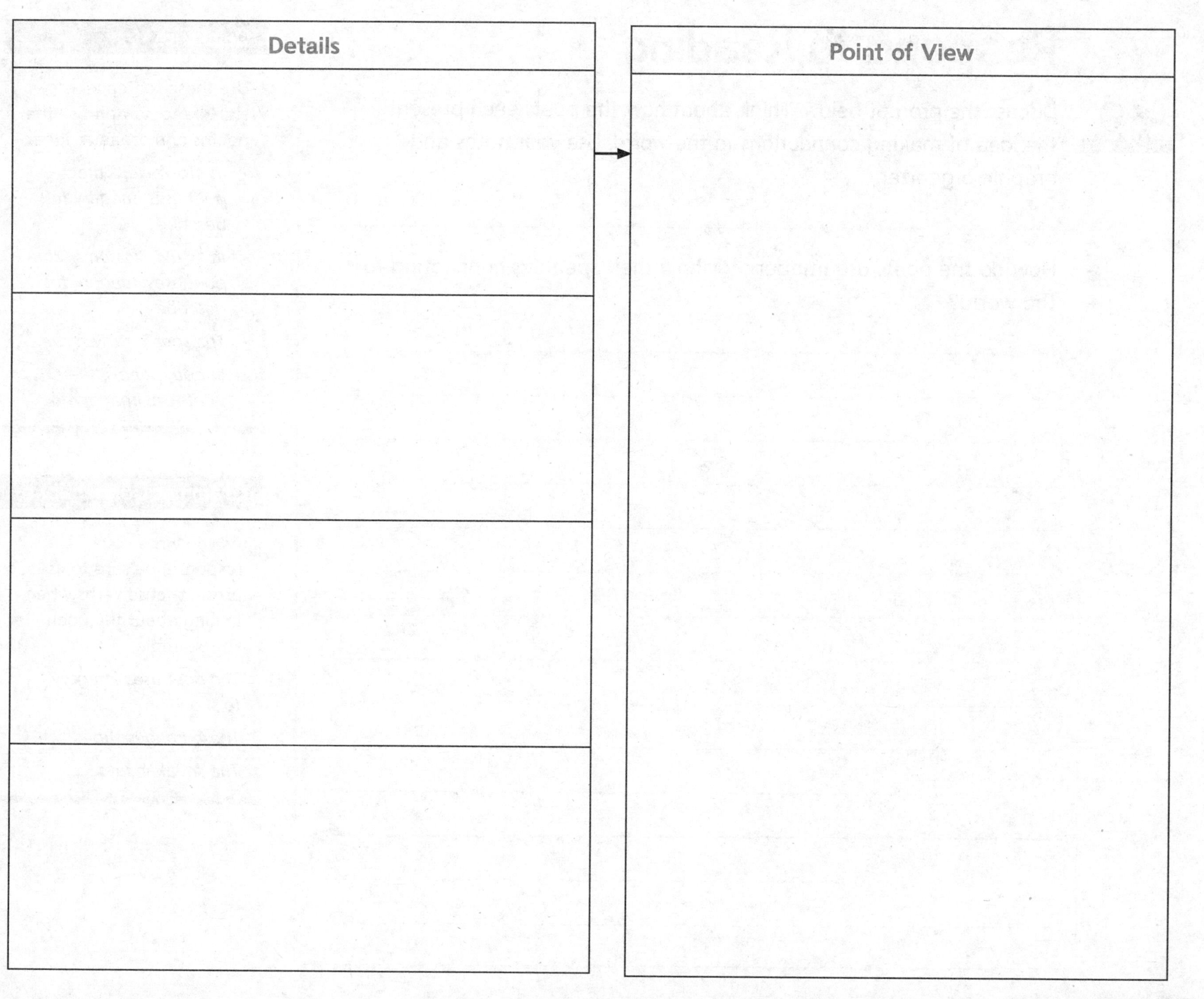
Details
Point of View

Respond to Reading

Discuss the prompt below. Think about how the poets each present the idea of making connections to the world. Use your notes and graphic organizer.

How do the poets use imagery to show their speakers connecting to the world?

____

____

____

____

____

____

____

____

____

____

____

____

____

____

Quick Tip

Use these sentence starters to paraphrase the poems and organize ideas.

- *In "To Travel!" the poet uses imagery to describe . . .*
- *In "Wild Blossoms," the poet uses imagery to describe . . .*
- *The speaker says . . .*
- *In both poems, the poets use imagery to . . .*

Grammar Connections

As you write your response, be sure to use present tense verbs when talking about the poem. For example:

*The poet **uses** imagery to show . . .*

*These images **show** . . .*

*The speaker **says** . . .*

Formatting an Email

An **email** is a good way to contact businesses, groups, or government leaders. An email has a standard format:

- To: (the email address you are writing to)
- Subject: (a word or phrase that identifies your email topic)
- the message telling why you are writing

How are an email and a letter alike and different? Write your answer.

____

____

Write an Email With a partner, create an email to send to an elected or appointed leader in local, state, or national government about an issue that is important to you. Be sure to use formal language. Use the following points to help you format your email:

- What is the issue that you want to address?
- Is the issue about something in your community, town, or state?
- Who is the best person to contact about the issue? Make sure to use correct salutation, or greeting, in your email. For example:

Dear Senator Smith:

Discuss how you will research your issue so you have accurate information to include in your email. After you complete your email, you will present it to your class.

School Crosswalk

To: andrea.ruiz@example.gov

Subject: School Crosswalk

Dear Mayor Ruiz:

We are students in Ms. Scott's fifth grade class at Madison Elementary. There is a busy crosswalk in front of our school. We would like information about getting a traffic light put at the intersection.

The sample email above shows the beginning of a message that describes a community issue.

Reread | ANCHOR TEXT

You Are My Music

Literature Anthology: pages 472-474

How does the poet use words and phrases to describe what Ana means to her sister, Aida?

Talk About It Reread the first and last stanzas on **Literature Anthology** pages 472–473. Talk with a partner about how Aida describes Ana.

Cite Text Evidence What details in the poem help you understand the connection between Ana's hands and her sister? Write text evidence.

Text Evidence	What It Tells About Ana

Write Aida describes Ana's hands ______________________________

____

____

____

Make Inferences

Pay attention to how Aida describes Ana's hands and what the hands are doing. Does she use words that are positive or negative? Paying attention to the feeling a word or phrase gives will help you infer how the speaker in a poem feels about things.

You and I

How does the poet use figurative language to help you understand her message?

Talk About It Reread the second stanza on **Literature Anthology** page 474. Discuss with your partner what "splits us each in two" means.

Cite Text Evidence What phrases help you understand the poet's message? Write text evidence and tell the message.

Text Evidence	Message

Write The poet helps me see the message ______________________

____

____

____

Quick Tip

Think about the subjects of the poem, *you* and *I*. How does the poet connect the two?

Evaluate Information

You can evaluate the details in a poem to determine its message. How does the poet present the message? Explain whether you agree or disagree with the poem's message.

Respond to Reading

Discuss the prompt below. Apply your knowledge of figurative language, such as the use of metaphors, to inform your answer. Use your notes and graphic organizer.

Think about the figurative language in the poems. How do the poets use it to communicate a message about people and the connections they make?

Quick Tip

Use these sentence starters to talk about and cite text evidence.

- *The metaphors in the first poem . . .*
- *The figurative language in the second poem . . .*
- *These techniques show that people can connect with each other by . . .*

Self-Selected Reading

Choose a text and fill in your writer's notebook with the title, author, and genre. Record your purpose for reading. For example, you may be reading to answer a question, or for entertainment.

Reread | PAIRED SELECTION

A Time to Talk

Why are the first two lines of the poem important to the poem's meaning?

Talk About It Reread the poem on **Literature Anthology** page 476. Discuss with your partner what the speaker is saying in the first two lines.

Cite Text Evidence What clues help you understand how the first two lines affect the rest of the poem? Write text evidence.

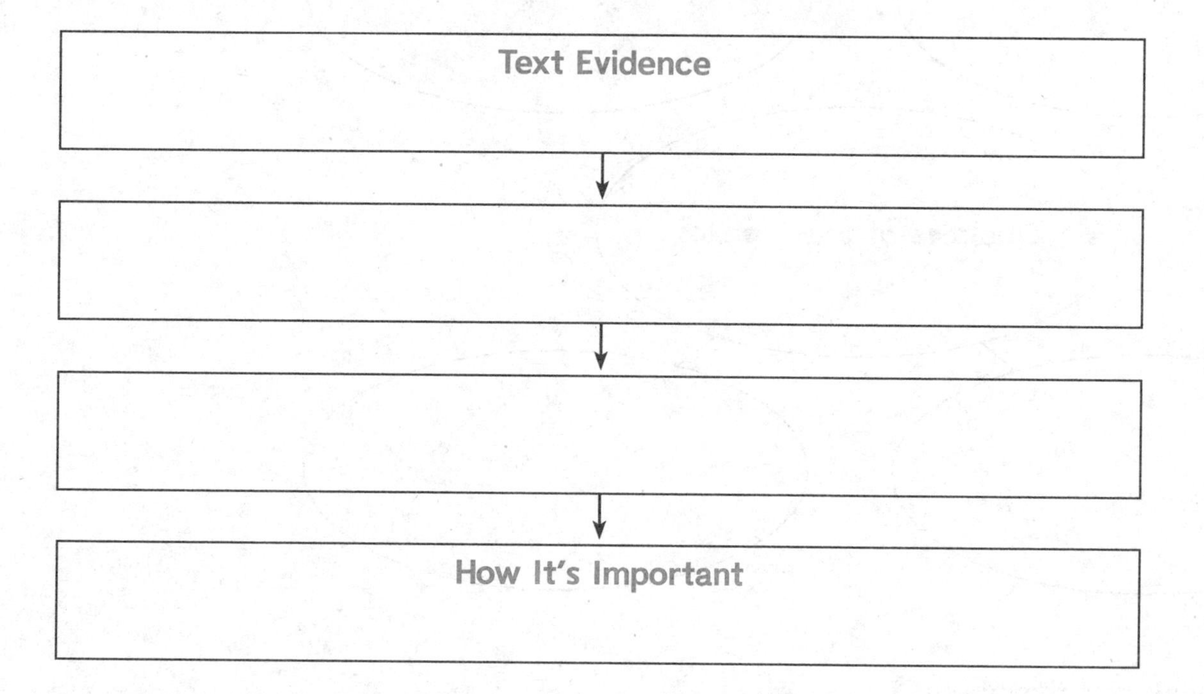

Write The first two lines affect the rest of the poem because ____

____

____

Quick Tip

Think about a time when a friend called to you. What did you do? Making connections to personal experiences may help you increase your understanding of a poem.

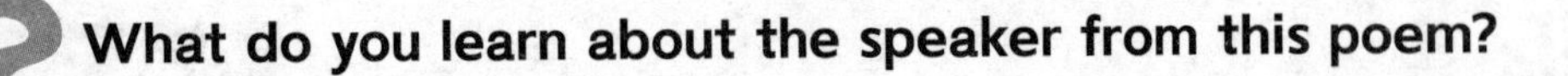

Reread | PAIRED SELECTION

What do you learn about the speaker from this poem?

Talk About It Reread the poem on **Literature Anthology** page 476. With a partner, talk about what choice the speaker of the poem has to make.

Cite Text Evidence What words and phrases describe what kind of person the speaker is? Write text evidence in the web.

Quick Tip

Think about the speaker's actions. What does this tell you about his or her qualities?

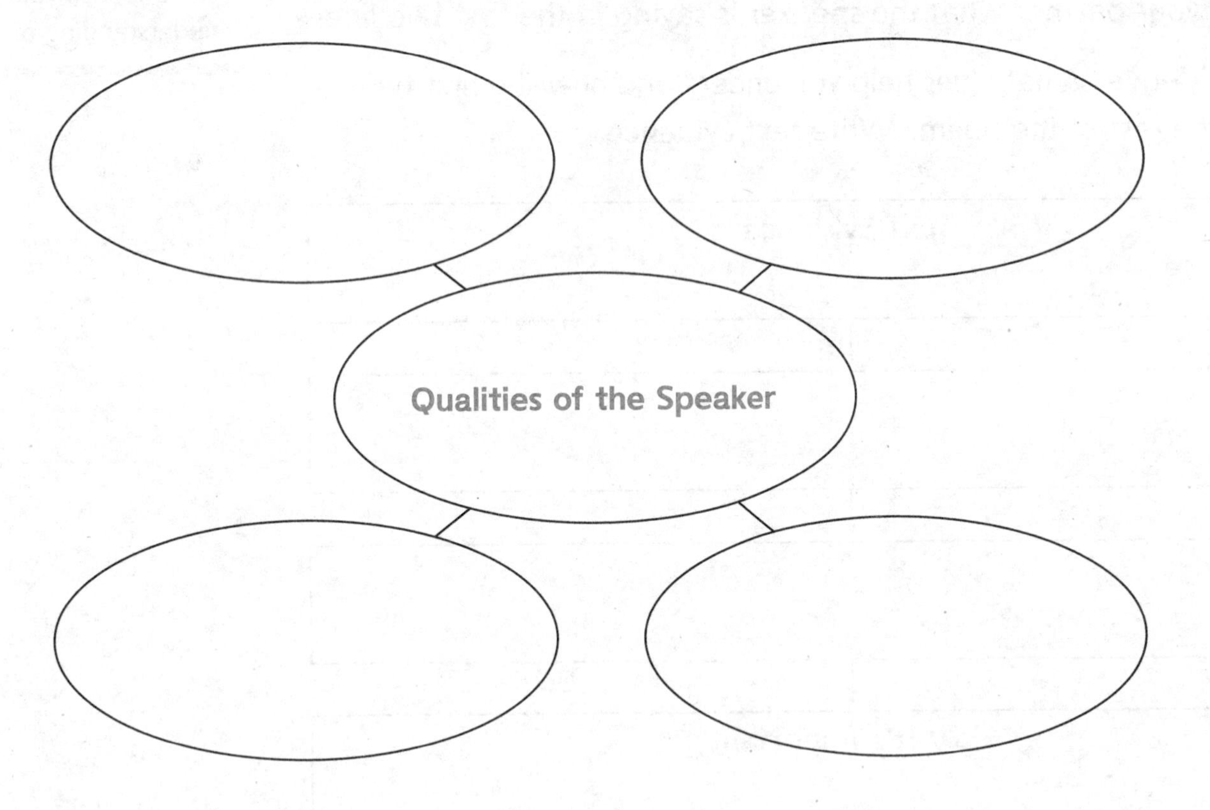

Write The speaker of this poem ______________________________

____

____

____

Imagery

Imagery is created by the words writers choose to describe ideas, actions, places, or things. Poets use imagery to create mental images for readers to deepen their understanding. Imagery can also appeal to the senses and create a mood, or feeling, in a poem or narrative.

FIND TEXT EVIDENCE

In "A Time to Talk" on **Literature Anthology** page 476, the poet uses imagery to create a scene in which a farmer stops work to talk to a friend. The poet uses vivid words such as *thrust* to show the action. The word *mellow,* as used here, means "soft" and gives a sense of what the ground is like.

> I thrust my hoe in the mellow ground,
> Blade-end up and five feet tall.

Readers to Writers

Choose precise words to create imagery in your writing. For example, if you want to create a vivid picture and feeling of an approaching storm, use sensory words such as *biting* or *chilling* instead of *cold* to describe the wind. A thesaurus will help you find just the right words.

Your Turn Reread lines 7–8 of the poem on page 476.

- How does the poet use imagery to help you visualize the hoe?

  ____

  ____

- What mood does the poet create in the last two lines of the poem?

  ____

  ____

CSP_schankz/Fotosearch LBRF/age fotostock

Text Connections

How are the connections made by Alfred, Lord Tennyson similar to the connections made by the poets of "You Are My Music" and "A Time to Talk"?

Talk About It Read the poem. Talk with a partner about what the oak tree symbolizes, or represents, in the poem.

Cite Text Evidence **Circle** words in the poem that help you visualize an oak tree. **Underline** words and phrases that compare the oak tree to a person.

Write The connections made by the poets are similar because ______________________

____

____

____

____

____

____

____

____

____

____

Quick Tip

Think about why Tennyson compares a person to an oak tree. This can help you compare this poem with the others that you have read.

The Oak

Live thy Life,
Young and old,
Like yon oak,
Bright in spring,
Living gold;
Summer-rich
Then; and then
Autumn-changed
Soberer-hued
Gold again.
All his leaves
Fall'n at length,
Look, he stands,
Trunk and bough
Naked strength.

– Alfred, Lord Tennyson

Expression and Phrasing

Before reading a poem aloud, think about the meaning of the poem. Then read with correct **expression** and **phrasing**, or prosody, to bring the poem to life. Exclamation points are clues for expressive reading. *Phrasing*, or grouping words into meaningful phrases, will also make the poem clearer. Note punctuation, such as commas, to help you with phrasing.

Quick Tip

When reading with expression, be aware of your rate or speed of reading. When expressing excitement, many people read a little faster, as well as louder.

Page 156

A novel waves her arms to me,
"Come read! Come read!" she cries.
Her pages dance with ancient tales,
A feast for hungry eyes!

The exclamation point is a signal to read the words with excitement.

Commas show a place where you can pause after a phrase.

COLLABORATE

Your Turn Turn back to pages 156–157. Take turns reading aloud the poem "To Travel!" with a partner. Think about how you felt when you first read the poem. Express these feelings in the way you read. Also use the punctuation to help you with phrasing.

Afterward, think about how you did. Complete these sentences.

I remembered to ____

____

Next time, I will ____

____

WRITING

Expert Model

Literature Anthology: page 474

Features of a Lyric Poem

A lyric poem expresses the personal feelings or thoughts of the speaker. A lyrical poem

- has a musical quality and may include rhythm, a regular pattern of sounds
- may include rhyme
- often contains imagery, including sensory language

Word Wise

Poets often use sensory language in lyric poems. Sensory language appeals to the five senses. This helps readers create a mental image while they read, complete with sounds, sights, and sometimes even smells and tastes. Read aloud the first two lines of "You and I." Think about the mental image they create of the speaker looking at the world.

Analyze an Expert Model Studying other lyric poems will help you learn how to plan and write a lyric poem of your own. **Reread** "You and I" on page 474 in the **Literature Anthology**. Write your answers to the questions below.

What feeling is the speaker expressing? What words tell you that?

____

____

____

How does the poet create a musical quality in the poem?

____

____

____

____

Plan: Choose Your Topic

Freewrite On the lines below, write about ways you have helped your community. Maybe you volunteered to clean up the classroom, raised money, or helped younger kids with their homework.

____

____

____

____

____

____

Quick Tip

You can use informal language when writing poetry. Choose words and phrases that best express the speaker's feelings about the topic.

Writing Prompt Choose one idea from your list. Write a lyric poem about the topic you chose. Remember to include some details about how you helped the community.

I will write my poem about ______________________________.

Purpose and Audience Think about who will read or hear your poem. Will your purpose be to inform, persuade, or entertain them? Then think about the language you will use to write your poem. How will you help your readers understand the speaker's feelings? Record your answers in your writer's notebook.

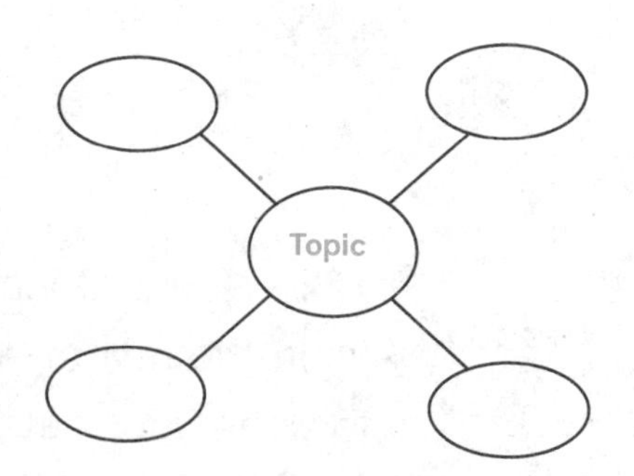

Plan In your writer's notebook, make a graphic organizer to plan the details you will include in your poem. Put your topic in the center.

Plan: Sensory Language

Brainstorm Descriptive Details Once you have chosen your topic, think of some details you plan to include. Then think about how to describe them. Sensory language is language that makes readers see, hear, taste, touch, or smell something. Be descriptive when you use sensory language. "I bit into a crisp red apple, tasting its tart juice" helps the reader visualize the speaker's experience more than "I ate an apple."

As you plan your first draft, ask yourself these questions:

- Am I telling readers something or am I showing them?
- Are the words I'm using related to any of the five senses?
- How might I use more descriptive details to make this part more interesting?

Think of two descriptive details you might use in your lyric poem.

1. ______________________________
____

2. ______________________________
____

Take Notes Once you have decided on the details you will include, fill in the rest of your graphic organizer. If you need more space to write your details, use a separate sheet of paper in your writer's notebook.

Draft

Rhyme Lyric poetry does not have to rhyme, but many lyric poems do. Rhyming can help give your lyric poem a musical quality. If you choose to write a rhyming poem, you will need to think about what kind of rhyming pattern you will use. In the example below from "Running," the second and fourth line rhyme.

> "Feet pound the pavement,
> Arms pump up and down,
> Sun's up and smiling,
> As I jog through the town."

Now use the verse above as a rhyming model to write a verse that could go in your lyric poem.

____

____

____

____

Write a Draft Use your graphic organizer to help you write your draft in your writer's notebook. Don't forget to use sensory language and descriptive details.

Quick Tip

If you are having problems coming up with rhyming words, you can use a rhyming dictionary. You can also try substituting different first letters for the word you want to rhyme. For example, change the "f" in *fun* to "p" and now you have "pun." To hear if your poem has a musical quality, try reading it aloud and tapping out the beat.

Revise

Concrete Words Poets can create mental images and make ideas clear for readers by using concrete words. Concrete words, such as *juicy* and *apple*, name things we can know through our senses. Abstract words, such as *love* and *courage*, refer to ideas. Read the lines below. Then revise them to improve word choice by deleting abstract words and replacing them with more concrete words.

I felt happiness about friendship.
The beach was a place of cleanliness, not trash.
Our time was well spent cleaning the shore.

Quick Tip

If you have trouble coming up with concrete words, close your eyes and think about what is happening in the poem. Give yourself a few moments. Then write down what you saw. Use this to add concrete details. Then, try reading your poem aloud.

Revision Revise your draft to improve word choice. Check that you have made your ideas clear by using enough concrete words and deleting any unnecessary abstract words.

Peer Conferences

Review a Draft Listen carefully as a partner reads his or her work aloud. Take notes about what you liked and what was difficult to follow. Begin by telling what you liked about the draft. Ask questions that will help the writer think more about the writing. Make suggestions that you think will make the writing stronger. Use these sentence starters.

I enjoyed this part of your draft because . . .

More concrete words or sensory language would help me visualize . . .

I have a question about . . .

This part is unclear to me. Can you explain why . . . ?

Partner Feedback After your partner gives you feedback on your draft, write one of the suggestions that you will use in your revision. Refer to the rubric on page 183 as you give feedback.

Based on my partner's feedback, I will ______________________________

____

____

____

After you finish giving each other feedback, reflect on the peer conference. What was helpful? What might you do differently next time?

Revision As you revise your draft, use the Revising Checklist to help you figure out what text you may need to move, elaborate on, or delete. Remember to use the rubric on page 183 to help you with your revision.

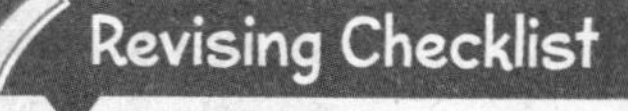

- ☐ Does my poem express the speaker's personal feelings?
- ☐ Does my poem have a musical quality or rhythm?
- ☐ Do I have enough sensory, descriptive details?
- ☐ Are there any abstract words that could be replaced or better described with concrete words?

Edit and Proofread

When you **edit** and **proofread** your writing, you look for and correct mistakes in spelling, punctuation, capitalization, and grammar. Reading through a revised draft multiple times can help you make sure you're catching any errors. Use the checklist below to edit your sentences.

Grammar Connections

When you proofread your poem, make sure that you have capitalized proper nouns, such as names and places if they have a specific title or name.

Editing Checklist

- ☐ If you used stanzas, is there space between the stanzas?
- ☐ Are all prepositional phrases used correctly?
- ☐ Are proper nouns capitalized?
- ☐ Are descriptive adjectives used correctly, including comparative and superlative forms?
- ☐ Are all words spelled correctly?

List two mistakes you found as you proofread your lyric poem.

1. ______________________________

____

2. ______________________________

____

Publish, Present, and Evaluate

Publishing When you **publish** your writing, you create a clean, neat final copy that is free of mistakes. As you write your final draft be sure to write legibly in cursive. Check that you are holding your pencil or pen correctly.

Presentation When you are ready to **present** your work, rehearse your presentation. Use the Presenting Checklist to help you.

Evaluate After you publish your writing, use the rubric below to **evaluate** your writing.

What did you do successfully? ______________________________

What needs more work? ______________________________

____

Presenting Checklist

- ☐ Stand up straight.
- ☐ Look at the audience.
- ☐ Speak clearly and reflect in your voice the musical quality of your poem.
- ☐ Speak loudly enough so that everyone can hear you.

4	3	2	1
• the poem clearly expresses personal feelings and ideas about the topic • includes sensory and concrete words to create an image in the reader's mind • has a successful musical quality	• the poem expresses personal feelings and ideas about the topic • includes sensory and concrete words to create an image in the reader's mind • has a musical quality	• the feelings and ideas expressed in the poem are unclear • uses few sensory and concrete words to create an image in the reader's mind • has an uneven musical quality	• the poem lacks feelings and ideas about the topic • uses few sensory and concrete words • has no musical quality

SHOW WHAT YOU LEARNED

Spiral Review

You have learned new skills and strategies in Unit 6 that will help you read more critically. Now it is time to practice what you have learned.

- **Cause and Effect**
- **Context Clues**
- **Make Inferences**
- **Point of View**
- **Imagery**
- **Theme**

Connect to Content

- **Find and Evaluate Sources**
- **"The Tortoise and the Solar Plant"**

Read the selection and choose the best answer to each question.

Animal ADAPTATIONS

1 Biologists study how creatures in the wild survive. Many animals, such as the walking stick, camel, and blowfish, have important adaptations to help them. Some adaptations are structural. Some adaptations are behavioral. Certain structures and behaviors are necessary for survival.

Walking Stick

2 The walking stick is a forest insect. It eats mostly leaves and resembles a twig. The walking stick ranges in length from half an inch to thirteen inches. Its cylindrical body may be covered with spikes, or bumps, and it mostly appears green, tan, brown, or gray. One function of the walking stick's structure is to provide camouflage, or a disguise, that helps it blend in with the surrounding environment.

3 Because the walking stick is hard to see, it is mostly protected from its predators. Animals that would eat it include birds, small reptiles, and rodents. If a predator happens to spot one, the walking stick will try to save its own life through different behaviors. It might play dead, detach a leg, or poke a predator with its spiny legs. When it feels threatened, the walking stick might shoot a bad-smelling liquid at its attacker.

Guenter Fischer/Getty Images

Camel

4 The camel is a desert animal that eats mostly plants. It may grow to be over seven feet tall and weigh up to 1,800 pounds. Its body may have one or two humps. Because the camel must survive long journeys in the desert where there is very little water, it has adapted so that it can survive for up to six months without water.

5 The camel's well-known hump is a structure that stores fat. This fat can be changed into water and energy. In addition, a camel sweats very little, so its body can hold onto water. Red blood cells help with a camel's blood flow during times without water. The camel is also able to open and close its nostrils to keep out blowing sand. Long eyelashes and hairy eyebrows help keep sand out of the camel's eyes. The camel also has big flat feet that keep it from sinking into the sand.

Blowfish

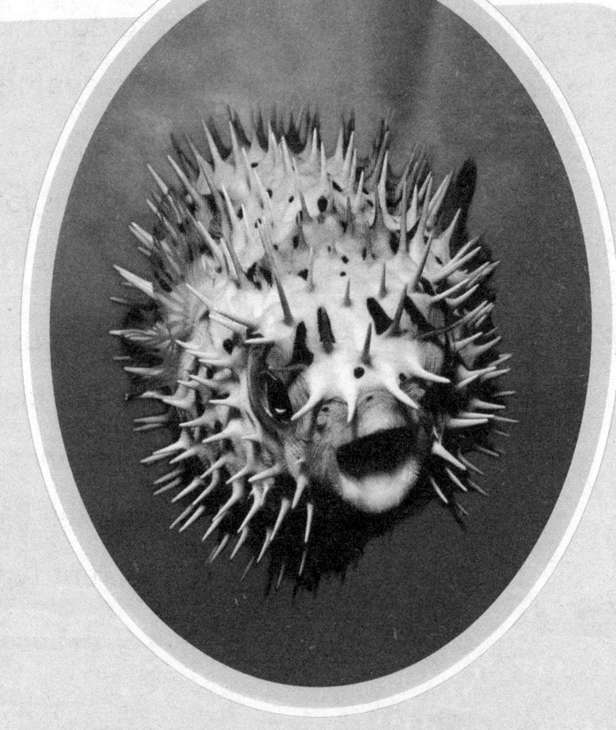

6 The blowfish, also known as the pufferfish, is found in the warm ocean waters of the Pacific, Atlantic, and Indian Oceans. It grows up to three feet in length. This fish feeds on algae and shellfish. Because the blowfish is a poor swimmer, it is easy prey for predators, such as tiger sharks and sea snakes. To make up for its lack of athletic ability, the blowfish has developed an interesting behavior.

7 When in danger, the blowfish fills its elastic, or stretchy, stomach with water or air. This allows the fish to grow several times its normal size in order to protect it from predators. In addition, the skin of some blowfish is covered with pointy spikes, and its body gives off a deadly and bad-tasting poison. These traits are key to a blowfish's survival.

SHOW WHAT YOU LEARNED

1. In paragraph 2 the word camouflage means —

   A function

   B structure

   C disguise

   D environment

2. Which adaptation is shown by the photo of the walking stick?

   F blending in with its surroundings

   G playing dead

   H detaching a leg

   J shooting a bad-smelling liquid

3. Why does the camel need to go on long journeys in the desert?

   A It needs to escape from predators.

   B It needs to search for water.

   C It needs to hunt other animals for food.

   D It needs to get rid of the fat in its hump.

4. Cause-and-effect text structure is used in paragraph 7 mainly to —

   F describe the predators of the blowfish

   G explain the physical appearance of the blowfish

   H explain the reason behind the blowfish's behaviors

   J show how to identify different types of blowfish

Quick Tip

For some multiple-choice questions, you may have to make inferences. Look for text evidence that supports your inference.

Read the selection and choose the best answer to each question.

CONNECTED

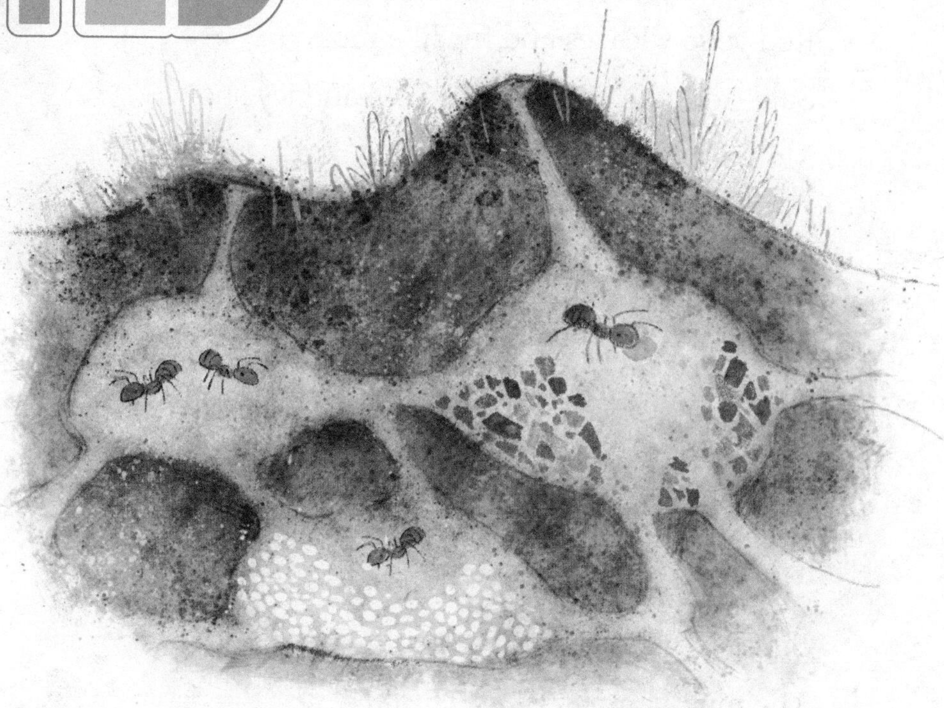

Below
Three damp hollow chambers
Kitchen, nursery, and bedroom
Elaborate dark tunnels burrowed between
5 One tiny worker ant heaves on its back
A grain of displaced brown earth
I'm careful to step around
Fearful of disturbing his work
A hill to make home.

10 Above
Cozy hollow cradled by a strong branch
Constructed of green grass and bendable sticks
Papery leaves, velvet moss, fringed feathers
Glued with sticky mud
15 Secret from sly predators
Safe from stinging rain and biting wind
I'm careful to tip-toe by
Worried over waking the chicks
A nest to make home.

SHOW WHAT YOU LEARNED

20 In the quiet forest
Hollowed rock
Cleared of debris, downy with warm bedding
Red-yellow leaves and fur-like moss
Safe from the bitter winter cold and icy snow
25 Mother bear settles in for a long nap
Pulls the young ones close
I'm careful to stay on the trail
Respectful of her territory
A den to make home.

30 In the noisy city
Cement foundation laid, wooden walls framed
Triangular roof trusses placed, shiny siding erected
Silver metal pipes and colorful wires hung
The man hammers—*tap, tap, tap*
35 The woman measures and saws—*whirr*
Laughing children try to stay out of the way
I'm careful to smile and wave
Happy for new neighbors
A house to make home.

1. This poem is written from the point of view of –
   - A a worker ant
   - B a construction worker
   - C a mother bear
   - D a respectful observer

2. Which of the following lines from stanza 3 includes imagery?
   - F Cleared of debris, downy with warm bedding
   - G Mother bear settles in for a long nap
   - H Respectful of her territory
   - J A den to make home

3. The repetition of the phrase "to make home" stresses the idea that –
   - A creatures enjoy being in nature
   - B creatures share a basic need for shelter
   - C creatures have difficulty caring for their young
   - D creatures follow routines

4. What is the theme of the poem?
   - F People should protect the environment so that animals can live safe and healthy lives.
   - G Living creatures are linked because they all build homes.
   - H Animals in the wild build very different types of homes.
   - J Shelters built on the ground are the safest homes.

Quick Tip

For multiple choice questions, read all the answer choices carefully. Then choose the best answer.

EXTEND YOUR LEARNING

COMPARE AND CONTRAST

COLLABORATE

- In the **Literature Anthology**, the historical fiction text *The Unbreakable Code* on pages 430–443 and the expository text "Allies in Action" on pages 446–449 show how different groups helped during World War II.
- List how each of these groups helped the war effort. Then compare and contrast and discuss with a partner how they were similar and different.

Navajo: ______________________________

Women: ______________________________

____

Mexican workers: ______________________________

African Americans: ______________________________

- Write a brief composition about one group's contributions.

ASSESS STEREOTYPES

A stereotype is an oversimplified opinion about a certain person, group, or issue. Critical readers pay close attention to texts and challenge stereotypes. Explain the purpose of this stereotype and how women during World War II proved it wrong: *Women were not able to do jobs typically held by men.*

Use text evidence from "Allies in Action," **Literature Anthology** page 447.

____

____

____

IDENTIFY SOUND DEVICES

Poets use words to create sounds that support meaning. Read this poem.

The spider ceaselessly spun
its smooth, silken thread
Many hours passed before it was done
Tick! Tick! Many hours passed before bed

The poet uses many sound devices.

- A lot of the words start with the letter *s*: *the spider ceaselessly spun its smooth, silken thread.* This is called **alliteration**, or the repetition of beginning consonant sounds. The words echo the action.
- **Rhyme** occurs when two or more words end with the same sound: *thread* and *bed.* A **rhyme scheme** uses a rhyming pattern.
- In the last two lines, the poet uses **repetition** with the phrase "Many hours passed."
- **Onomatopoeia** is the use of a word to copy a sound, such as *tick, buzz,* or *thud.*

Find another poem that uses these sound devices. In the chart below, list an example from the poem and note what kind of sound device it uses.

Poem	Example	Sound Device

EXTEND YOUR LEARNING

FIND AND EVALUATE SOURCES

SOCIAL STUDIES

When researching a historical topic, you can use primary and secondary sources. A **primary source** is a document, such as a letter, created during the time period by someone who participated in an event. A **secondary source** is a document, such as an article, created after the time period by someone who did not participate in the event. When reading primary and secondary sources, evaluate them for credibility.

- Talk about one of the groups cited in "Allies in Action" on pages 446–449 of the **Literature Anthology**.
- Locate one primary and one secondary source that provides information for how this group helped the United States during World War II.

Use the checklist below to confirm the credibility of each source.

Checklist

- ☐ Who published the source, and is the publisher reputable?
- ☐ When was the source published?
- ☐ Who is the author? Did the author cite his or her sources?
- ☐ Do the sources contain relevant, factual information?

The primary source is (circle one) credible/not credible because ____________

____

The secondary source is (circle one) credible/not credible because ____________

____

THE TORTOISE AND THE SOLAR PLANT

Log on to **my.mheducation.com** and reread the *Time for Kids* online article "The Tortoise and the Solar Plant," including the information found in the interactive elements. Answer the questions below.

- Look at the map. In what states is the Mojave Desert?

____

- The prefix *trans-* means "across." Based on this and clues in the selection, what does the word *transmission* mean? How does it relate to the example in this article?

____

____

____

- Why did construction of the solar plant suddenly stop after the government approved it?

____

____

____

- What point of view does the author express in the conclusion of the article?

____

____

Time for Kids: "The Tortoise and the Solar Plant"

A desert tortoise

Fuse/Getty Images

TRACK YOUR PROGRESS

WHAT DID YOU LEARN?

Use the rubric to evaluate yourself on the skills you learned in this unit. Write your scores in the boxes below.

4	3	2	1
I can successfully identify all examples of this skill.	I can identify most examples of this skill.	I can identify a few examples of this skill.	I need to work on this skill more.

☐ Theme
☐ Homophones
☐ Cause and Effect
☐ Context Clues
☐ Point of View
☐ Personification

Something that I need to work more on is ________________ because

____

____

____

Text to Self Think back over the texts that you have read in this unit. Choose one text and write a short paragraph explaining a personal connection that you have made to the text.

I made a personal connection to ______________ because ____________

____

____

____

Present Your Work

Discuss how you will present your email to your class. Use the Presenting Checklist as you practice your presentation. Discuss the sentence starters below and write your answers.

When I was planning my email, I learned ______________________

____

____

____

I would like to know more about ______________________

____

____

____

Quick Tip

When you begin your presentation, provide your audience with information on the issue you chose to write about. Share your research experience and any follow-up plans for your email.

Presenting Checklist

- [ ] Decide how you will divide your presentation with your partner.
- [ ] Rehearse your presentation. Provide feedback to your partner.
- [ ] Speak slowly and clearly during your presentation.
- [ ] Make eye contact with your audience.
- [ ] Allow time for questions. Listen carefully and provide complete answers.